Eden Prairie
The First 100 Years

By
Helen Holden Anderson

A Project of the
Eden Prairie Historical Society
and
The Eden Prairie Historical and Cultural Commission

Printed by Viking Press
7000 Washington Avenue South
Eden Prairie, Minnesota

Sketches and Cover Design
by
Dale Redpath

CONTENTS

Introduction

The year was 1851. A treaty in which the Mdewakanton Sioux gave up their land west of the Mississippi River was signed. In a short time the flowering prairie along the Minnesota River in the future town of Eden Prairie was settled.

In St. Paul, women and children with their personal belongings were put on side-wheelers for the trip up the Minnesota River to Bloomington Ferry or Hennepin Landing. The men drove the livestock west along the Indian trails. Some folks, carrying all their earthly possessions on their backs, came by way of the Minnetonka Trail, turned south and staked claims in the wooded area of northern Eden Prairie known as Little Switzerland.

These people put down roots, their own and those of crops. They felled trees, built log houses, barns, churches and schools. A community named Eden Prairie was formed and governed by a town board. Time passed. Soon huge barns and large rambling farmhouses dotted the landscape. It became an area of yellow grain and red clover fields, apple orchards and raspberry patches, with large herds of cattle grazing on the hillside. This agricultural life had its rewards, for the farmer had a place of his own where he could do the work of which he could be proud. He could achieve relative security and derive happiness from sharing work and ideas with his neighbors.

This was Eden Prairie for more than one hundred years. But suddenly a change took place. All that had been built was swept away. It came so fast many hardly realized what had happened. Economically, the farmer could not maintain his former way of life and signed away his life's heritage to the new man on the scene—the developer. There was a feeling of lost identity when the "home place" was known by the name of a new development.

In an address delivered to the Old Settlers of St. Anthony and the Pioneers of Hennepin County in 1872, Dr. Edward D. Neill, the Minnesota historian, began by saying, "Whenever we witness growth (such as we have seen in Eden Prairie) we desire to know something about what it was in the beginning. In all ages men have looked back with reference to the origin of things and compared the time that was with the present—the then with the now."

Thus, in the 1960s, the idea of a local historical society was born. If our local history were to be preserved it would have to be now, for there were only about a half dozen people of the second generation and maybe two dozen of Eden Prairie's third-generation families still living in the area.

The Eden Prairie Historical Society was organized as a non-profit organization in June, 1969. Since its beginning, an extensive research on local history has been carried on. Fortunately, many of Eden Prairie's first residents took time to record in stories, letters and diaries much of the early history. Important information was found in the collections assembled by the Minnesota Historical Society and the Hennepin County Historical Society. Added history was gleaned from the newspapers that for many years carried Eden Prairie news: the Hennepin County Review and the Shakopee Argus.

Some of the most interesting programs of the society have been on family histories—for families make history. One member of the family was always willing to research, write and present the family history. These meetings turned out to be large family reunions. Many of these histories have been included in this book. No doubt, there are many more families still living in Eden Prairie who have equally interesting accounts locked up in their memories. The stories found in this book should be thought of not as the total history of Eden Prairie but representative of the total. If one family is highlighted while another is not, it may be that descendants of that family took time to record and provide information while others did not. Also, many family members are mentioned only in reference to their specific actions or interesting events in which they were involved. This book is not a definitive history of Eden Prairie. It is but a minute part of the memories, ideas, and attitudes of people during the first one hundred years of Eden Prairie's settlement and growth.

This book, in part, is an oral history of Eden Prairie. I have listened and taped living memories of many who have lived here since birth. It was a refreshing experience, for it is one thing to write that this is the way things were but it is another thing to hear someone tell how he or she recalled it because he or she was there. I want to extend a special thanks to my many Eden Prairie friends who so enthusiastically cooperated in these personal interviews.

For more than one hundred years Eden Prairie was a farming community governed by a township board. This all changed in 1963 when Eden Prairie became a village and now a city. This is a story of the revolutionary changes in the lives of its people and its land. We live in the present, but also in the past and the future. The past is simply a stepping stone to the future. We cannot ignore or separate ourselves from its importance, for without the remembrance of the past there is little appreciation of things today.

Helen Holden Anderson

Acknowledgments

A great part of this book is made up of living memories. These memories tell what it was like to grow up in Eden Prairie and they form the backbone of this story about our community.

I am grateful to the following people for providing the Eden Prairie Historical Society with written histories of their families: Margaret and John Bren, Esther Moran Hessing, Dean Holasek, Phyllis Rogers Kopesky, Arthur Miller, Nell Schmeidel Nesbitt, David Pavelka, Dwight Picha, and Iona Raguet.

I want to thank the people who provided information through written material, casual conversations, and taped interviews. They are: Calvin Anderson, James Brown, Elizabeth C. Bryan, Mildred Clark, Dorothy Raguet Doughty, Priscella and Howard Good, Eva Klima Hirt, Carol Quam Hone, Allene Hookom, Frances Jerabek, Helen Goodrich Mastin, Arthur Miller, Louise Tessmer Mitchell, Linda Brekke Mona, Marion and Ralph Nesbitt, Emil Pauly, Abbie and Albert Picha, Homer Raguet, Marion Rogers, Diane Dredge Simons, Elmer Tobias, Harold Unze, and Beatrice Glenn Venness.

Two of Eden Prairie's young people were very helpful. They are Dale Redpath who did a number of sketches and the cover design and James Rannow who photographed historic sites.

I wish to thank the Historical and Cultural Commission for the City of Eden Prairie for providing the funds needed for the printing of this book. The members are: Carol Quam Hone, chairperson, Judith Ellingson, Jeannette Harrington, Allene Hookom, Albert Picha, Mary Upton, city staff member Sandy Wertz, and myself.

Finally, I want to thank my husband, Calvin. His encouragement and support were essential to the completion of this project. We have felt for some time that the material gathered by the Historical Society and my own research in local history should be shared with the people of the community. It is therefore our desire to make a gift of the copyright rights to the City of Eden Prairie, Minnesota with the understanding that any profits from the sale of the book will go into a fund for the preservation of Eden Prairie's history.

Helen Holden Anderson

IN THE BEGINNING

Home of the Mdewakanton Sioux

The first explorers found Minnesota to be a wilderness of great forests, wild grassy prairies, extensive waterways and the land of the Dakota Indian. These people traveled the waters by canoe, lived off the animals and plants of the forest and called this their undisputed homeland and hunting ground.

This mighty Dakota nation was divided into tribes who were divided into bands. The band that is of interest to us is the Mdewakanton Sioux, who lived on the shore of Mystery Lake (Lake Mille Lacs) which was the home of the Great Spirit. Annually, all the Dakotas in that area gathered at Mystery Lake. It was a time of uniting the Indian bands and a time to renew their union with the Great Spirit, the giver of life. When the solemn rites and the tribal dances ended, all departed to their own area in the great forest feeling once again they had fulfilled their sacred duty. Thus, they lived year after year unaware that conditions outside their realm would someday completely disrupt their way of life.

The great forest that covered the northeastern part of our continent was called the home of the Woodland Indians. The Woodland Indians comprised many tribes, most of whom had the same customs and beliefs, and spoke the same language, the Algonquin tongue. One branch was a tribe called Ojibway or Chippewa. From tribal tradition and archaeology we have learned they once lived along the Atlantic sea coast. As the eastern part of our country became settled, they started moving westward up the St. Lawrence River, then along the Great Lakes, finally reaching Lake Superior. There they found it profitable to deal with the French traders who gave them traps, guns and knives in exchange for the beavers they trapped. Large numbers moved farther west into the forests of northeastern Minnesota, the land of the Dakotas. They gave these proud people the nickname Sioux, which, in the Chippewa language, means "snake in the grass."

The Sioux resented this invasion of their hunting ground but their spears, bows and arrows were no match for the Chippewas with their guns and steel knives. They were soon forced out of the northern forests. The Chippewas then advanced to the sacred ground of the Mdewakanton Sioux band on Mystery Lake. This invasion was furiously resented and never forgotten.

The Mdewakanton Sioux wandered south and ultimately settled along the Minnesota River. Years went by but there was no peace between these mighty Indian tribes. The Sioux kept sending war parties into Chippewa country and the Chippewas raided the Sioux camps in return. A dividing line between the Sioux and the Chippewa lands was drawn in 1825 at a grand conference held at Prairie du Chien, Wisconsin, by tribal leaders, Indian agents and representatives of the United States government. This boundary was not honored and did not stop the fighting. There were always young braves who wanted to fight for revenge or glory. On May 27, 1858, the last battle between these two tribes in this area was fought on Eden Prairie soil at Murphy's Ferry on the Minnesota River.

The Mdewakanton Sioux who lived in the area of Eden Prairie were happy and content in this land of lakes and streams. With bone hooks and spears they caught fish and turtles. Flocks of wild geese, ducks and other aquatic birds settled on the lakes, while the muskrat, beaver and mink lived along the shores. Wild berries, plums and roots were enjoyed in season and stored for winter. Cranberries that grew in profusion in the lowlands around the lakes were gathered in the fall. Wild rice was plentiful in the bottomland lakes along the Minnesota River. Sugar was not only taken from the maples but from the birch, ash and boxelder as well. The woods abounded in wild game. In the fall moccasined feet led them along the narrow Indian trails to the hunting grounds for deer and buffalo. For the Mdewakanton Sioux it was "Wa-se-cha"— the land of plenty.

3

Prehistoric and historic history reveal Indian mounds on the river bluffs of the Minnesota River in the southern part of Eden Prairie. According to archaeologists, there were nine groups of burial sites on the bluffs overlooking the river. In the 1800s there were 238 burial mounds, but now there are only 48 known—some round and others oblong in shape. These are in the area of Dell Road, Eden Priarie Road, Flying Cloud Airport and Riverview Road. Only an archaeologist with a knowledge of Indian mounds would be able to locate them.

According to Jonathan Carver, an early explorer, the custom of these imaginative people was to place their dead upon stagings overlooking lakes, rivers or exceptionally beautiful scenery which they enjoyed while they were living. They would leave them there for a certain period of time when the parched bones were buried in mounds with the other members of the family. The pioneer and his plow, highway construction crews and home builders have destroyed most of these sacred mounds.

Slowly the land of the Sioux began to change. Civilization was creeping in along the river. The area east of the Mississippi River had been opened for settlement by the Treaty of 1827. Opening the land west of the river seemed inevitable. From the day the first territorial governor, Alexander Ramsey, arrived in May, 1849, there wasn't a day in which he was not strongly urged to take whatever steps necessary to acquire the land of the Sioux west of the river. The Sioux did not want to give up their villages in the comparative shelter of the bottomlands and the broad valley of the Minnesota River. They did not want to be pushed west into the bleak and open prairie where the winds were strong and the winters cold. They knew this area from their fall buffalo hunts. But they accepted the inevitable and signed away their land at the treaties of Traverse des Sioux and Mendota in 1851.

The Indians had been ordered by their chiefs to rendezvous before their removal to the government reservation on the upper Minnesota River. The night before leaving, they danced to forget their sorrow and to fortify their hearts. All night long the pounding of drums could be heard, torches flared, painted bodies pranced and voices shouted beneath the quiet stars. In the morning they departed, following the trail through the big woods to the west. As the last travois scraped loosely across the western boundary, oxen plunged over the eastern edge. Breaking plows screeched through the tough, resistant sod, and smoke rose from open fires.

Although the Sioux had been ordered to the reservation and although they did, in fact, live there through many winter moons, they still felt that they had every right to visit their ancient home and the graves of their forefathers. But when they came back they found the white man's farms now encircled the lakes and that the white man objected when the Sioux pursued his game across the cultivated fields. There was the question of the wild rice marshes and the cranberry bogs. Did the white man feel it was right to keep them all for himself? These grievances, along with the government failing to meet its annuity payments, led to the uprising of 1862 and the Indians being completely gone from this area.

For the Indian some of the pioneers had little patience. The Indian was seen as being in the white man's way; of not fitting into his plans. The Indian was seen as being lazy and having more curiosity than any other human being, often frightening people by peeping through cabin windows or quietly opening doors and peering over the shoulders of the women before his presence was discovered. Their ways were strange and often hard to understand. Living and getting along with the Sioux in Eden Prairie are best told by the first pioneers who lived among them.

Indian Stories

Mrs. Robert Anderson (1827–1924), from "Autobiography of Mary Jane Hill Anderson," written in her ninety-fifth year for her children:

I came in 1853 with my husband and small children and settled in one of the first log houses built in Eden Prairie. We paid for our farm from the cranberries which grew in a bog on our land and which sold for one dollar a bushel.

I had never seen Indians before and so was very much afraid of them. One day a big hideously painted brave marched in, seated himself and looked stolidly around without making a sound. His long knife was sticking in his belt. I was overpowered with fright and for a moment could do nothing. My children, one a two-year-old and the other a baby, were asleep behind the curtain. Realizing that I could do nothing for them and that his anger might be aroused if he saw me run with them, I fled in the direction where my husband was working. I had run about a quarter of a mile when my mother heart told me I might not be in time if I waited for my husband, so I turned and fled back towards the cabin. Entering, I saw my little two-year-old boy standing by the Indian's side playing with the things in his belt while the Indian carefully held the baby in his arms. In his belt were a tobacco pouch and pipe, two rabbits with their heads drawn through, two prairie chickens hanging from it by their necks, a knife and a tomahawk. His expression remained unchanged. I gave him bread and milk to eat and ever after he was our friend, oftentimes coming and bringing the children playthings and moccasins. When he left, he gave me the rabbits and prairie chickens and afterwards often brought more game.

Mrs. Mary Staring Smith, from "Old Rail Fence Corners" (1914):

When we first came to live in Eden Prairie I thought I had never seen anything as beautiful as that flowering prairie. In the morning we could hear the clear call of the prairie chickens. I used to love to hear it.

Harvesting wild rice. Water color by Eastman, about 1850. Indians of Minnesota, Minnesota Historical Society.

Sioux Tepees were cone-shaped structures of skins stretched over a framework of poles. Photo taken about 1900. Indians of Minnesota, Minnesota Historical Society.

There were great flocks of them and millions of passenger pigeons. Their call of "pigie! pigie!" was very companionable on that lonely prairie. Sometimes when they were flying to roost they would darken the sun, there were so many of them. Geese and ducks were numerous too. Blackbirds were so thick they were a menace to the growing crops. I used to shoot them when I was twelve years old.

We had a cow named Sarah. She was a lovely, gentle creature. Mr. Anderson brought her up on the boat. My dog was an imported English setter. These and an old pig were my only playmates. I used to dress my dog up but when I found my old pig would let me tie my sunbonnet on her I much preferred her. She looked so comical with that bonnet on lying out full length and grunting little comfortable grunts when I would scratch her with a stick.

I never saw such a sad expression in the eye of any human being as I saw in Otherday, the Sioux friend of the whites. It seems as if he could look ahead and see what was to be the fate of his people. Yes, I have seen that expression once since. After the massacre when the Indians were brought to Fort

Little Crow, the Sioux Chief who led his people in the bloody Sioux Uprising of 1862. Portrait by Mayer, 1861; Indians of Minnesota.

Sioux Indians moving to a new camp site. Water color by Seth Eastman, about 1850. Indians of Minnesota, Minnesota Historical Society.

Snelling I saw a young squaw, a beauty, standing in the door of her tepee with just the same look. It used to bring tears to my eyes to think of her.

There used to be a stone very sacred to the Indians on Alexander Gould's place near us. It was a red sandstone and set down in a hollow that they had dug out. The Sioux owned it and never passed on the trail that led by it without squatting in a circle facing it, smoking their pipes. I have often stood near and watched them. I never heard them say a word. They always left tobacco, beads and pipes on it. The Indian trails were worn deep like cattle paths.

At the time of the Indian outbreak, refugees came all day long on their way to the fort. Such a sad procession of hopeless, terrified women and children. Many were wounded and had seen their dear ones slain as they

Burial Scaffolds. Photograph by D. F. Barry, 1870. Indians of Minnesota, Minnesota Historical Society.

7

A Sioux woman drying meat and boiling bones for marrow fat. She is pounding some of the dry meat with berries and tallow to make pemmican, which was used when meat was scarce. Sketch by Frederick N. Wilson, Indians of Minnesota, Minnesota Historical Society.

fled to the cornfields and tall grasses of the prairie. I'll never forget the expression on the faces of some of those poor creatures.

Mrs. Frederick Penny, from "Old Rail Fence Corners":

We lived about four miles from Shakopee, at what was called Eden Prairie. My father was William O. Collins. The Sioux Indians' old camping ground and home was on the river bottoms at Shakopee. Three miles below our place was Hennepin Landing where the boats landed coming from St. Paul. The trail of the Sioux led directly past our house, so we saw a great deal of the Indians.

One thing we were taught was to never show fear of the Indians. They knew very quickly and loved to scare anyone who showed they were afraid. Chaska and five of his men had been out duck hunting and stopped at our house for supper the night before the outbreak of 1862. The Indians were always friendly with all members of my father's family and never asked for a meal unless they were willing to pay with ducks or in some way. The next morning after Chaska had supper with us, a man came riding from St. Peter telling everyone to flee. Twenty families (ours among the others) remained.

One day on my way to school, I heard the children calling me to run, but the grass was so high I could see no one and did not know an Indian was near. When I saw him, I was not afraid. I went to the schoolhouse door but the teacher was so frightened she had locked the door and I could not get in. I stood waiting and the Indian patted me on the head and said, "Heap brave papoose" and went down the trail.

Miss Sara Faribault, from "Old Rail Fence Corners":

My father, Oliver Faribault, built a house which was his home and trading post near "Little Six" of Shakopee's village in 1844. It was a fine point for a trading post, as three Indian villages were near: Good Road's, Black Dog's and Shakopee's. He

Red Rock, "Home of the Great Spirit". on the Indian trail west of Red Rock Lake.

was a very successful trader. I can well remember the great packs of furs. We used to play all around the country near the post. I could shoot an arrow as well as a boy.

We used to go often to the sacred stone of the Indians and I have often seen the Sioux warriors around it. There was room for one to lie down by it and the rest would dance or sit in council around it. They always went to it before going into battle. They left gifts which the white people stole. I can remember taking a little thing from it myself. I passed a party of Indians with it in my hand. One of the squaws saw what I had and became very angry. She made me take it back. She seemed to feel as we would if our church had been violated. This stone was stolen by a man from the east and taken there. This loss made the Indians very angry.

The Indians did not understand the white man's ways. When the white man had a big storehouse full of goods belonging to the Indians and the Indians were cold and hungry, they could not see why they could not have what was belonging to them, if it would keep them warm and feed them. They could not see why they should wait until the government told them it was time for them to eat and be warm. It was the deferred payments that caused the outbreaks. This is what I often heard from the Indians.

One morning in the summer of '58 we heard firing on the river. Most of the Sioux had gone to get their annuities but a few who were late were camped near Murphy's Ferry. These had been attacked by a large band of Chippewa. The fighting went on for hours, but the Chippewa were repulsed. That was the last battle between the Sioux and Chippewa near here.

I have often seen Indians buried on platforms elevated about eight feet on slender poles. They used to put offerings in the trees to the Great Spirit and also to keep the evil spirits away. I remember that one of these looked like a gaily colored umbrella at a distance. I never dared go near.

Myron S. Staring, from the Minneapolis Journal, *May 12, 1915, "Pioneer Tells of Fight Between Chippewa and Sioux":*

Fifty-three years ago a war party of twenty Chippewas, out to revenge themselves on the Sioux of Shakopee's band, fought a desperate battle at Murphy's Ferry. This fight was witnessed by two settlers in Eden Prairie from the crest of the bluff overlooking the Minnesota River and the ferry. One was Philip Collins, who had seen service in the Mexican war and afterward became a soldier of fortune serving through the Civil war and various South American revolutions. The other was Myron S. Staring, now a sedate real estate dealer in Minneapolis.

"It was just about daybreak when I was awakened by the sound of firearms down toward the ferry, and having some young horses down on the Minnesota bottoms, I hurried out to look for them. As I went in that direction I met Philip Collins who was searching for some stock to drive away from

This marker was removed during the construction of Highway 169 in 1924.

danger. When we reached the crest of the bluff bordering the Minnesota valley we saw the Indians below us. Most of them were under cover. The Chippewas tried to rush the Sioux several times, but without success. I think that they were afraid to fire low for fear of hitting the white people across the river, who had come down from Shakopee to see the fight.

"Both sides loaded and fired as rapidly as they could, all the while whooping and yelling like maniacs. About 10 a.m. the Chippewas retreated from the field and went north towards the Mississippi river. The Sioux then rushed out and took the scalps and the squaws followed and mutilated the bodies. They cut off the head of a young chief and took it to their village. I understand that Neill gives the name of this chief as Noonday, but I think possibly this is a mistake, as the only Noonday I ever heard of was a Sioux. The young chief was one of the handsomest and most stalwart Indians I have ever seen.

"After the battle I counted fifteen Chippewas in the narrow strip of land between the two lakes. One of the Chippewas was so badly wounded that he died and was buried near Glen Lake.

"How many the Sioux lost I don't know, as they refused to tell. They took away their dead, but my brother-in-law, Dr. J. W. Daniels, stationed at the Sioux agencies, told me that several had died up there from wounds received in the fight at Murphy's Ferry.

"The chief of the Sioux was Shokpay, or Little Six, from whom the present town was named. I knew him well, in fact, I knew all the members of his band and often attended their dances and councils. Naturally I talked Sioux almost as readily as English.

"Shokpay was a wonderful orator and his fame has not been exaggerated in the least. His eloquence in council had a tremendous influence. Little Crow, the leader of the uprising of 1862, I also knew well. He was a good speaker and not a bad sort of a fellow, but not as fine a man as Shokpay.

"I don't want to defend the Sioux for the uprising, but they had great provocation. It must be remembered that they were mere savages and they knew no other way to resent the wrongs upon them than the way they had adopted against all their enemies from time immemorial."

Mrs. Robert Anderson, from "Autobiography of Mary Jane Hill Anderson":

In the spring of 1862 James Anderson had a log raising to build his barn. For some reason I did not go, and as I was timid about staying alone, Mrs. Brewster, a widow who was like a fairy godmother to us all in time of need stayed with us. About eleven o'clock, Ezra Paine, a boy about eleven years old came to the door and said, "I was sent to tell the Anderson settlement that the Indians have broken out on the frontier and are killing people and burning the houses and villages. The men were to meet at one o'clock at the Gould schoolhouse to decide whether to build a fort at Eden Prairie or go to Fort Snelling for protection."

I told him to go over to the log raising to tell the men there, which he did after I had offered to go part way with him to show him the way through the woods. Of course there were very few roads at this time—mostly cow paths. Late in the afternoon we began to look for Father to come home, and we had the table set and the kettle boiling. It grew dark and he did not come. Then we put the children to bed, with their clothes on. We took turns standing outside, listening for his footsteps. At ten o'clock he had not come. Mrs. Brewster came in and said, "Oh, Mary Jane, the Indians are coming. Shakopee is on fire! What shall we do?"

I happened to remember that James Gamble was not very well, and probably was not at the log raising, so I said, "Let us take the children and go over to Gambles." We took them up and started; but before we went Mrs. Brewster, thrifty soul that she was, said, "Maybe after all we had better pick up the dishes. The cat might break them." "Oh, never mind," I replied. "We may never be in this house again." And so we went out into the moonlit woods, fear in our hearts lest the Indians should be lurking in the shadows. We heard a footstep, and hid in the bushes, but a familiar cough announced the approach of Father. He took the baby out of my arms, turned its little face up to the moonlight and said, "Thank God, dear, they may kill your body, but they cannot kill your soul."

This was not very reassuring to my already overstrained nerves, and as we went home I had such a bad nervous chill that I could hardly walk. When we reached home the singing of the kettle on the stove welcomed us. How many times that old teakettle (a heavy iron one, by the way) ministered to our needs. They bathed my feet, as my teeth still chattered, and Mrs. Brewster made a cup of tea, but I was still deathly sick. Realizing that my condition needed to be dealt with gently but firmly, Father shook me and said, "Mary Jane, where is your faith? They can't do anything but what the Lord permits them to do. Brace up now and take this tea and you will feel better."

Then Father told why he was so late coming home. It had been decided at the meeting at the schoolhouse to send William and Robert Brewster and William Anderson on horseback in the direction of the trouble to learn the truth about the report. As they had not returned at night it was feared they had been killed, so Father left some of the men at the schoolhouse, hoping against hope for the return of the boys. Late in the night they did return, with the report that there was a little trouble, and several had been killed, both Indians and whites. The story had grown. There was some uneasiness on the part of the settlers because the Indians were beginning to resent their coming. In many cases the white settlers were at fault.

Oh, I forgot to say that the fire which Mrs. Brewster thought was Shakopee burning was only a straw stack.

James Stewart, from the Hennepin County Review, November 7, 1929:

It was the year of the Indian Outbreak of 1862 when I came up the river from St. Louis with my parents, the John Stewarts.

I was just a baby at the time but as I grew older I heard the stories of that outbreak many times. One entire family was wiped out except for an eight year old boy who hid under pumpkin vines in the field. Many women and children went to Fort Snelling for safety. My wife's uncle, George Frederick, was one who cut the ropes at the execution of 38 Sioux at Mankato. His entire family had been murdered.

I was married to Emma Mitchell in 1889 by Rev. Samuel Pond of Shakopee who married most of the early settlers on the prairie, including my wife's parents, the Samuel Mitchells, who came in 1854.

Speaking of weddings, I remember an Indian wedding celebration held not far from Shakopee that lasted an entire week where the white people in the neighborhood were as active as the Indians in enjoying the dancing and feasting.

We made our home on the southside of Red Rock Lake near an Indian campground. One of our rarest relics is a pipe-stone pipe which lay in the ground for over seventy years according to the judgments of the oldest settlers and probably was the property of Chief Red Rock whose grave was located on our farm. Indians came every year to mourn the death of their chief and each year painted red a large rock which marked his grave. The body of this Sioux chieftain was moved to the area of Birch Island Lake north of Glen Lake about 1890 after the historic red rock had been stolen from our farm.

The side-wheeler "Favorite" a passenger and freight steamer on the Minnesota River, about 1860. Minnesota Historical Society.

The River

Today it is hard to visualize that the quiet, twisting waterway that forms our southern boundary once bore large steamboats and barges vital to the settlement of Eden Prairie and the land to the west.

The Minnesota River, known as the River Warren in geological history, has been here for more than ten thousand years. It was the southern outlet for Lake Agassiz, that vast, ancient lake that covered the Red River region at the closing of the glacial period. This turbulent river varied in size from one to five miles in width and from seventy to two hundred feet in depth until the northern ice wall broke, opening a second drainage channel to the sea through the Hudson Bay. As the ice age waned, the water receded, leaving the beautiful river bluffs and the rich, fertile land known as the Minnesota River Valley. To get an idea of the river's expanse, one should stand on the river bluffs in Eden Prairie and look south over the broad valley to the hills in the distance. Those hills were the south bank of that mighty river.

For untold generations the only craft this river bore was the canoe of the Indians. Then came the French traders with their retinue of voyageurs. Mackinow, or keel boats, laden with Indian merchandise plied constantly along the river's length. These boats were propelled by men and poles. They were from twenty to fifty feet in length with sides five feet high. Along the tops were fastened heavy planks on each side for walkways. A small, low cabin for the cook was built in the stern and during bad weather a tarpaulin was spread over it. The crew consisted of a captain, who also was the steersman, ten pole men, and the cook. The crew could make from five to

Minnesota River Steamboats at St. Paul, about 1862. Minnesota Historical Society.

fifteen miles a day depending on the stage of the water, sandbars and the number of rapids they had to climb.

This river was known to the Indians as the Wattapaw Menesotor (Minnesota); to the French traders it was St. Pierre; and the English called it St. Peter. Through an act of Congress, Henry Sibley, the first governor of the state, had it registered by its Indian name, Minnesota.

People were eager to explore that rich valley to the southwest, along which the covetous eyes of the white man had long gazed with prying curiosity. In 1850, the Mississippi river boat, Anthony Wayne, arrived in St. Paul with a party of St. Louis people. It was a jolly crowd which, to enliven their trip, had brought with them a small band for dancing. It was suggested to the captain that, to entertain his guests, he take them on an excursion up the Minnesota River; then little known to the outside world. On June 28, 1850, with the decks crowded with 114 of St. Paul's prominent citizens plus the seventy St. Louis people, they started up the Minnesota River.

The points of interest after leaving Fort Snelling were the Indian villages of Black Dog, Cloudman, Good Roads, Little Six (Shakopee), and at Chaska the village of the Wahpahton Sioux. When the steamer reached the rapids at Carver, it turned around for the journey downstream. A month later, the riverboat Yankee, with the Sixth Regiment band from Fort Snelling aboard, pushed up river for more than 150 miles. This trip was described as being equally gala.

Soon, steamboats with such expressive names as Time and Tide, Black Hawk, Excelsior, Iola and Equator were steaming up the river. Nothing was more uncertain than one of these steamboat journeys on the Minnesota. The best boats had to stop and gather wood for fuel in riverside forests. Their smokestacks frequently were demolished by overhanging bows or their hulls

were punctured by snags. These mishaps caused the passengers to while away hours on the banks, telling stories, hunting, or picking wild berries. The captain and the guests took it all in good humor.

During the fall and winter following the Indian treaties of 1851, there was a great rush of settlers into the Minnesota River Valley. Before the spring of 1852 a series of townsites lined the banks of the river from St. Paul to the mouth of the Blue Earth, a distance by water of 150 miles. These embryo towns were in dire need of communication with the outside world. The swarms of settlers ever pressing westward needed supplies. But after the settlers were established and had become producers the export of farm products became important business. By 1860, wheat had become the principal export of the valley. At the St. Paul Wharf in 1862, there were 413 arrivals of steamers that had made round trips on the Minnesota.

As the need for freight transportation in the valley became increasingly greater, there was a large increase in the use of barges. Instead of carrying freight in the large steamers, it was found to be more expedient to carry strings of barges drawn by small tugboats.

The appearance of the first boat in spring brought relief from the loneliness of winter. The whistle of the boats was a signal for men, women and children to drop everything and rush to the hill or down to the levee to exchange greetings with the captain and his crew. The narrowness of the river made it easy to form friendships with the men on deck. Many people felt they lived more intimately with the steamers on the Minnesota than they might have on another river.

The brisk river commerce came to almost a complete halt when the Northwestern Railway reached New Ulm. Just a few steamboats and barges continued to travel the river until 1897.

14

HENNEPIN.

Hennepin County

Surveyed and drawn by J. H. Case

As the area became more populated, the river changed. The settlers unwittingly frustrated the river. Cultivation of the prairies absorbed the moisture that once had drained off the ancient sod into the springs and streams that once fed the river. The early settlers in Eden Prairie, who watched the boats and barges from the river's bluff and knew the river in its prime, are now gone. Only recorded history holds the secret of this river and its importance in the settlement of Eden Prairie and Minnesota.

The Ghost Town of Hennepin

They called it town-site fever. Along with the pioneers came the land speculators. Many of the towns envisioned by the speculators never got off the planning board. Of the towns that did get started, many were platted; lots were sold; stores, blacksmith shops, and hotels were built. Many of these towns were at river landings where the steamboats dropped off people and freight. With the coming of the railroads, these towns just folded up. But these towns are of interest as they show the hopes and ambitions of the early settlers to develop this territory, as well as demonstrate man's innate courage and perhaps foolishness in his unending search for new frontiers of wealth.

In the spring of 1851, John H. Holmes, with John H. McKenzie, Emerson Shunway and David Apgar, loaded a flat boat with provisions and building materials and ascended the Minnesota River to the hollow at Teen-tah-o-ton-wa (Shakopee's village). Here, he erected a trading post and started trading with the Indians. Holmes is remembered as the founder of the town of Shakopee.

John H. McKenzie, who also had this town-site mania, took a claim in 1852 across the Minnesota River in sections 34 and 35 in the future township of Eden Prairie. Thinking this a good location for a town, he associated with the Honorable Alexander Wilkins, who at that time was secretary of the territory. They platted a portion of McKenzie's claim into village lots and called the embryo city Hennepin.

Eight other men were drawn into this adventure: James A. Case, Ramsey County surveyor; J. Van Eton, manager of Wilkins' land office; George Becker, lawyer, builder of railroads and the first state railroad and warehouse commissioner; and Charles Willis, lawyer, and later a district judge. There were three land speculators in the group: C.L. Filmore, Miras Abbott and Calib Lovering.

Without a doubt, the detailed plat of the town was modeled after the town sites in the East and probably occupied the long and lonely winter evenings of J.H. Case, who had surveyed the town site. On the plat all lots were numbered, the streets and boulevards were named. There was a seminar square plus two public squares. The plat was registered in Ramsey County, Territory of Minnesota in June of 1853. Later, it was registered in Hennepin County, May 17, 1854.

Although records show that Col. John H. Stevens, the founder of Minneapolis, built the first house west of the Mississippi in 1849, platting of lots in that area did not take place for some time as the land was still in the military reserve. This is the reason the men who platted the town of Hennepin felt it was to be the big city west of the Mississippi.

Records show there was a store built by Dunn and Howe, a gristmill, a sawmill, a blacksmith shop and a warehouse by the ferry. There were a number of houses and a hotel on the river bluff. The prairie above the town produced abundant crops of grain. Dr. E.D. Neill, in his History of Hennepin County, states that more grain was shipped from Hennepin Landing than any other location in the county. Piles of cordwood and hay were piled on the wharf and taken down river by the barges operated by Peter Ritchie, who also ran a ferry across the river.

Why was the town destined to fail? The location was a factor with the high bluffs to the north. The proximity to the towns of Shakopee, Chaska and Carver, which were situated on level ground, prevented its growth. There was the panic of 1857 when currency depreciated, business was paralyzed, real estate became valueless and many land speculators packed up and went back East. This was the time of the first grasshopper plague and the farm crops were poor. Then, the people who came to this area wanted land to farm and live on permanently.

When the Minneapolis-St. Louis railroad was built in the northern part of the township in 1871 and the Hasting-Dakota (Milwaukee) in 1881, shipment of grain and other produce went by rail.

All that remains to remind us of this town are the very early surveyor's maps, the plat of the town found in Plat Book 2, page 29, at the Hennepin County Government Center, and accounts left by historians.

Elizabeth Fry Ellet

In August, 1853, a distinguished authoress, Mrs. Elizabeth Frey Ellet, arrived in St. Paul. She was accompanied by a Miss

MRS. E. F. ELLET.
TAKEN IN 1850

Elizabeth Fry Ellet.

Clark, a widely known writer of that time. Mrs. Ellet visited the wilds of this area at the request of M.Y. Beach, editor-in-chief of the New York Times, a man of great prominence in the literary world and a contemporary of Horace Greeley.

Mrs. Ellet was a lively little lady who stood among the foremost female writers in America of that day. She and Miss Clark visited Lake Minnetonka just three months after it had been explored and named by Governor Ramsey in 1852. They proposed names for many of the bays and points on the lake and were the first to describe to the world its great extent and beautiful scenery.

These ladies also took a trip up the Minnesota River. Mrs. Ellet described the area as the "garden spot of the territory." They also climbed the river bluff to the upper prairie at the time of year when the virgin prairie was in bloom. Mrs. Ellet was overcome by the beauty of the prairie flowers and stated that the Garden of Eden could not have been more beautiful. When Mrs. Ellet returned to St. Paul she informed the officials there that she had just returned from the "Garden of Eden" and that this area should be called Eden Prairie.

The result of Mrs. Ellet's visit to our territory was the publication of two delightful books: "Pioneer Women of the West"(1852) and "Summer Rambles in the West"(1853).

Eden Prairie — Lakes and Streams

When the area west of the Mississippi was opened for settlement Eden Prairie was considered one of the most beautiful and picturesque in the county. Its southern border was washed by the Minnesota River. A panoramic view of the entire Minnesota River Valley could be viewed from the crest of the river bluffs that ran the length of the river in Eden Prairie.

The southern section of the township had a fine, natural prairie bordered on the west by the "big woods." North of the prairie the land was beautifully undulating, about equally divided between prairie and timber, making it good agricultural land. To the extreme north were the high hills and low valleys. The first settlers in this area rightly named it Little Switzerland.

The lakes and streams in Eden Prairie became known by the people who settled on their shores.

Anderson Lakes: Mrs. Robin Anderson, with eight of her eleven children, came up the river from Galena, Illinois. Each preempted land in the area around these lakes. The Andersons were Ulster-Scots from County Cavan, North Ireland.

Staring Lake: Jonas Staring, a captain on the Erie Canal, came to the Minnesota Territory in 1854 and built the first frame house in Eden Prairie on the south shore of the lake that bears his name. The lake was called Caroline on the 1860 map of Eden Prairie. Caroline was the name of Staring's wife.

Lake Riley: Patrick and Matthew O. Riley came from Ireland in 1845. In 1853 they preempted land on the north and east side of the lake that bears their name. On the 1860 map of Eden Prairie the name Bradford is also given. A William Bradford preempted land on the south shore of the lake.

Mitchell Lake: David Mitchell came from Monaghan County, North Ireland in 1852. He staked a claim on Mitchell Lake. This land was sold to the Miller brothers—Fred and John—in 1870. David Mitchell and his seven children lived in the central part of Eden Prairie.

Neill Lake: This lake was named for Aaron Neill, who came up the river from Galena, Illinois in 1850.

Bryant's Long Lake: The first maps of Eden Prairie show this lake as Island Lake. Alvin Holasek, whose grandfather bought land on the north side of the lake in 1857,

recalls his father telling him that it was called Island Lake because of the submerged island in the lake which was considered the best fishing spot on the lake. When the water was low the rocks on the island could be seen. Thus came the name of the area, Rock Isle Park. This lake is best known by the name Bryant's Long Lake, after William V. Bryant, who settled on its shores in 1852. He was a descendant of William Cullen Bryant, the poet.

Red Rock Lake: There was a red rock, held sacred by the Sioux Indians, on the west shore of this lake. The Indians used to sit in council around this rock, which was on the Indian trail going north, before and after their battles with the Chippewas.

Birch Island Lake: An Indian trail passed by this lake and the Indians had a camp among the birches beside it. Indian mounds have been found in this area.

Round Lake and Duck Lake: There are no records of how these lakes were named. Art Miller does remember when the soldiers from Fort Snelling held their summer maneuvers on the east shore of Round Lake in the early 1900s. As a boy, he would sit and watch the long caravan of horses and wagons pass the Miller's general store on County Road 4. His father furnished the camp with necessary supplies. Art remembers the death of one soldier. This young soldier foolishly was riding his horse in the lake when the horse stumbled. The soldier fell off and was kicked by the horse.

Grass Lake: The first maps of Eden Prairie show this lake as Tirrell Lake, after Judge Chesley B. Tirrell who came from Maine and preempted land in southern Eden Prairie.

Rice Lake: Here is where the Indians gathered their wild rice.

Purgatory Creek: The source of this creek is in the springs near where the Seven High Shopping Center is today. It meanders through the entire length of Eden Prairie, finally flowing into the Minnesota River. This stream has been known by three names, each determined by the area it flowed through. At its source it was called Purgatory Creek. Mrs. Anna Simmons Apgar, in 1854, gives this account of the name in "Old Rail Fence Corners":

"When our six families got to the springs near Excelsior, it was near dark and we struck the worst road we had found in this swampy land. The mosquitoes were dreadful, too. How dreadful, no one to-day can ever believe. One of the tired-out men said, "This is Hell!" "No," said another. "Not Hell, but Purgatory." Thus the stream was named. New settlers were always asked if they had come by the way of purgatory.

There was a grist mill built in 1861 in central Eden Prairie just north of where the creek flows under Pioneer Trail. The people in that area called it Mill Creek.

The people who lived near the town of Hennepin called the creek, Hennepin Creek.

Riley's Creek: This stream flows through the land preempted by Patrick and Matthew O. Riley in 1853.

Nine Mile Creek: This stream flows through the northeastern part of Eden Prairie on its way to the Minnesota River. The Old Shakopee Road crossed Nine Mile Creek in central Bloomington. The early French settlers in this area called it Neuf Milles Riviere (Nine Mile Creek) as it was just nine miles from Fort Snelling to this crossing.

Miller's Spring on Spring Road: When the brew made of birch bark, balsam, and wintergreen berries or the fires of spruce and resin prepared by the medicine man failed to heal the sick, the braves carried their loved ones to this spring of "minewaucan" (curing water). One only had to drink deep and often of this and the sparkle would return to one's eyes, the flush to one's cheeks,

Miller's Spring.

strength to one's limbs, and laughter to one's lips. January, the moon of difficulty, and February, the moon of sorrow, found many Sioux camped in the hollow of the hill by this spring.

The spring was on the Indian trail and future road to Shakopee. Here the farmers stopped to water their horses and quench their own thirsts.

Indian Trails: The Eden Prairie Historical Society has a copy of an 1860 map of Hennepin County which shows the Indian trails (inside the front cover of this book). The trails through Eden Prairie went between bodies of water on their way to either Fort Snelling or the Minnesota River. These trails were the first roads the pioneers used to get into the interior. A close study of this map shows that most of the roads through Eden Prairie were built along these Indian trails.

19

Murphy's Ferry: The Indians crossed the Minnesota River in their birch bark canoes, but the settlers demanded a better way to make the crossing. In 1856, the Territorial Legislature passed a law of particular interest to the settlers in both Eden Prairie and Shakopee. It granted to Richard G. Murphy the exclusive right for fifteen years to operate a ferry across the Minnesota River at a point known as Murphy's Landing. County Road 4 at that time was called the Murphy Ferry Road as it went down to this landing.

Richard Murphy was a colorful individual. He had fought in the Black Hawk War and in 1832 was elected to the legislature. In 1848, President Polk appointed him Indian agent in the Territory of Minnesota. When he served as agent to the tribes of Chief Redwood and Chief Yellow Medicine, he settled in Eagle Creek, just east of Shakopee. Here he built a large, two-story combination residence and stage-hotel. It soon became a mecca for travelers—a location for good food and drink, merry dancing and fresh horses.

Murphy was a good businessman and unfailingly collected his fare in midstream. He took no chances on having a customer whip his horse and take off before he could collect on the banks of the river.

In 1880, the first bridge across the river was built and was called the St. Lewis Bridge. The present bridge at Holmes Street in Shakopee was built in 1928.

A Home in a New Land

Historians have written about the causes of the great migration to America. They say the famine in Ireland, the revolution in Germany and the political oppression in other lands drove the people here. There was another influence that some historians feel may have been the greatest factor that made the people decide to leave the old world and seek the new. This force was the "letters from America."

Although many Europeans had heard of the wealth and opportunities in America, certainly few of the common folk had any first-hand information. But when a son left home and made the trip across the big ocean to the New World, this changed. Many months after his departure the parents would receive a letter, which was an event of great excitement. It was read and re-read. As more letters arrived from America, they were printed in the local papers. These letters contained the answers for the great dream of the poor. In America all men were equal and even a poor man could be a land owner and possess a home of his own.

"Going to America" was talked about in the marketplace, in social circles and on the levee. It became the challenge of the adventurous young and healthy who felt it provided the possibility for new opportunities and was a means of escape from unhappy conditions. Interest in farming in our area was aroused by James M. Goodhue's newspaper, Minnesota Pioneer. Beginning in 1850, Goodhue began writing enticing descriptions of the land west of the Mississippi River—making it sound most appealing to the farmers from the East and immigrants from Europe who often received a copy of his paper as they got off the boat.

The Indian treaties had been signed and the land west of the Mississippi had been opened for settlement. News of the fertile prairie flowed out to meet this inward-flowing tide of immigrants. As the Indians watched, these new arrivals unloaded their wagons, broke their ground, planted hasty crops and gathered wild hay. To the newcomer, it seemed incredible that so much land should run free. Rich and limitless it stretched, beautiful to the eye and the farmer's touch. The fresh and mealy earth crumpled in his eager hand with a promise of abundance.

Few who arrived in the summer bothered about a cabin until fall. But by then friendships were made and men went from claim to claim to raise logs while the women roasted meat in open fires and spread their best upon crude outdoor tables. Although the government survey had not been made, each settler selected a desirable piece of ground and marked it off by putting notches in trees or plowing a ditch with a homemade plow driven by a team of oxen. They built small cabins near the edge of a meadow on a southern or eastern slope so they were sheltered from the cold north wind and had the warmth of the southern exposure. Water came from the lakes and streams until a well could be dug at the edge of the meadow. All newcomers who reached a new settlement were welcomed into these first cabins. Practically every cabin sheltered from one to several families at a time until they could get a place of their own. There are records of families who were taken in for not just a few days but for months while they were getting established and building their own homes.

It required a willingness to endure poverty and to fight the elements in order to survive in this rugged and untamed wilderness. But the frontier also had its charm. The settlers were probably as contented in their crude cabins with plain surroundings, coarse clothing and homely fare as we are with the conveniences of our day. There were happy days, a cordial social life and charming simplicity. But there were always some who felt the pioneer life was too rugged to justify the land's opportunity and went back East.

The first settlers had great anxiety regarding the future titles to their lands. The government responded by passing the Preemption Act of 1841. The essence of the preemption law was that a claimant could move onto public land from which an Indian title had been cleared. Areas of 160 acres or less were stepped off or roughly measured in units of 40 acres. By occupation and improvement of the land, the settlers secured a prior claim to possession which they might assert when the land was surveyed and offered for public sale at $1.25 an acre. The land office at Washington and Ames in

Minneapolis was opened in 1854. Many claims were changed in size after the government survey. Disputes over boundaries resulted. Some had more and some had less than they had marked off. Records show that all the land in Eden Prairie was preempted by 1855.

The settlers had to watch their lands carefully and always have someone living on it at all times or some greedy and callous land grabber would use every excuse to seize it and the fruits of the pioneers' first labor. To take care of this problem, the Protective Claim Association was organized. Stringent rules were adopted against claim jumpers and others who might interfere with claims. The severe measures taken by the association were of such a character that no one who would attempt to jump a claim could be sure of his life.

Pioneer Stories

Here is a list of a few of the first families in Eden Prairie: From the area of Tyrone, Monaghan and Cavan in North Ireland came settlers with the names Anderson, Brown, Mitchell, Gamble, Clark, Steenson, Hill, O'Connell, McCoy, Lucas, Neill, Moran, Morley, Glen, Ritchie and Riley. From the eastern states came a group with the names Collins, Paine, Cummins, Staring, Curle, Tirrell, Bryant, Cornwell, Smith, Jarrett, Rankins, Hulbert, Goodrich, Pemberton, Gould, Raguet and Hankins. In western Eden Prairie were a number of German families: Seiler, Rouse, Lenzen, Miller and Pauly. The northern part of Eden Prairie was settled by people from Bohemia who had come to join their friends and relatives in the Minnetonka-Hopkins area.

When the immigrants arrived in New York, they found that the most comfortable route to this area was by way of the Albany-Buffalo Railroad and the Michigan Central railroad to Chicago, then to Galena, Illinois and up the Mississippi River to St. Paul. The expense of this trip from New York to St. Paul was from $25 to $28.

Pioneer Women: Mrs. Robin Anderson (Elizabeth) and her daughters. Top row: Fannie Mitchell, Bessie MacCraigue. Bottom Row: Ann Jane Brown, Sarah Gamble, Elizabeth Anderson and Martha Ritchie.

From the Anderson Genealogy, by Truman J. Beggs:

Joesy Anderson of Paisly, Scotland, was a merchant in and around 1575. On his travels to the continent, he met John Knox, the Scot founder of the Presbyterian Church in exile in Switzerland. The John Knox letters provide clues to the close friendship between the two men and without a doubt account for the Presbyterian heritage of the Eden Prairie Andersons.

Joesy Anderson's son, Archie, in 1602 enlisted in one of the Scottish Yeomen regiments and was sent to North Ireland where he remained, settling at Sixmilecross, County Tyrone. This began the line of the Ulster-Scot Andersons.

Robert Anderson was the first member of the family to come to Eden Prairie, followed by his brother, James. Shortly after his arrival, Robert Anderson's father, Robin, died. His mother sold their grist mill and tuck (flax fabric) mill and brought her family to America. There were eleven children. Three remained in Galena, Illinois. The five boys in Eden Prairie were Robert, James, Archie, Samuel and William. The three

girls, Sarah, Ann Jane, and Fannie, all married into families that had come from the same area in North Ireland. Sarah married James Gamble, Ann Jane married James Brown and Fannie married John Mitchell.

All the Anderson boys preempted large areas of virgin land. Their mother, Elizabeth Anderson, acquired many acres for herself and also for her children who were not of age.

The Andersons had large families. Their children had large families and so on it went. The farms were kept in the families, passing from father to son. It was a common saying that one could not step on ground in the eastern half of Eden Prairie that didn't belong to an Anderson or a close relative. Today there are only three Andersons in Eden Prairie that own lots on this ancestral land: Calvin Anderson, Topview Road; Willard Anderson, Flying Cloud Drive; and Kenneth J. Anderson, Gerard Drive.

Mrs. Robert Anderson, from The Autobiography of Mary Jane Hill Anderson:

In the spring of 1853 John Mitchell, Robert's uncle, came down from Minnesota to buy cattle. He was one of four men who,

Mary Jane Hill Anderson
(Mrs. Robert), age 95.

with their families, had settled about 25 miles west of St. Paul. By this time all the best homesteads around Galena had been taken, so he persuaded Robert to go to look at land in Minnesota. Robert went up that very fall by Mississippi River boat. Finding a 160-acre tract that looked desirable, near Eden Prairie, he staked it out. He left money with a man there to start building a log cabin, because it was necessary to make some improvements on a claim in order to hold it. Then he returned to Illinois for the winter.

In the spring of 1854 Robert and I started for our final destination on American soil, with a little money, seven cows, one sheep, a sow with a litter of pigs, a plow, a harrow, seed oats and corn, and quite a store of provisions—groceries, flour and hams. We had three children now, too: John, who was

nearly four; Robert James, two; and Samuel, only three weeks old. I was urged not to take the journey with so young a baby, but I did not want to stay behind.

Our trip upriver was uneventful. At St. Paul Robert put the children and me and our possessions on a very small steamer which plied the Minnesota River to Bloomington Ferry. He stayed behind to drive our livestock from St. Paul. Our boat was so small that freight had to be distributed carefully or it would tip over. Frequently the passengers had to run from one side to the other to balance it. Several times on that short trip the boiler sprang a leak, causing panic among the passengers. It was patched up as well as possible each time with bags of sand tied around the break. After many delays the boat reached Bloomington Ferry three and a half days after we started. There, the children and I debarked. The boat went on as far as Shakopee, but on the return trip it sank. Wasn't that a narrow escape for us.

At Bloomington Ferry, the children and I stayed with William Chambers, who owned the ferry and was married to Martha Mitchell, Robert's cousin. When Robert arrived with the stock, he got a wagon, took William's oxen, and drove us to the home of Billy McCoy, a friend living in Eden Prairie, about a mile from our unfinished log cabin. This was in April, and Billy McCoy, with the kind generosity of the early settler, urged us to stay with him and his family until we could get some crops in and then finish our home.

After the crop was planted Robert sold two cows for a hundred dollars, which was a good price then. With this money he bought lumber, windows and doors to finish our log cabin. The house had one room, with a loft which was reached by a ladder. Afterward we had a kitchen built on. We put in the little furniture we had brought with us and acquired a few more pieces. With our feather beds, dishes, and a small cookstove, we were quite comfortable. At first we divided the room in two with a curtain, making a living room and bedroom. Later we built a partition. We lived in that log cabin for 18 years, and seven children were born there.

Here, I think, were our happiest days. We had a home of our very own; we were young and hopeful; and with our little family and with life before us, and always work to do and the strength to do it, what more could we ask?

One day a couple of men came to our cabin and asked, "Who lives here?" When Robert told them, they said, "Oh, so you're the Andersons. You aren't going to hold this land. Our colony is going to settle here." Robert said, "No, I've claimed this for my relatives, and I'll hold it for them until they come in the spring." "Well," said the man, "we can bring a thousand men and we'll drive you and your relatives away." "All right," answered Robert, "bring your thousand men. I'll be ready for them. I'll promise you won't take a thousand away." This must have convinced the stranger, for they never came back.

The government surveyors came that summer of 1854, so we knew just where our boundary lines ran and where our 160 acres lay. Robert had intended to take all the heavily timbered land, but he couldn't do that and have the meadows, too. So he gave up part of the heavy timber to his brother James's claim, and took a 40 acre tract with a big meadow.

The next year the land was put up for public sale, and you had to pay the $1.25 an acre to the government if you wanted to keep it. The sales were made at the land office in Minneapolis. To get the title to our farm we had to go to the courthouse as soon as we could after the sale was posted and show that we had improved the land and that we were living on it—that was called proving up—and make the payment. I went to Minneapolis with Robert for this. It was necessary to leave home in the night, for it was a long, slow trip with the oxen. It took us until nearly noon, and when we got to the courthouse there were a great many settlers ahead of us, all waiting to prove up and pay for their land.

When our business was completed, we started back. Darkness was coming on by then, and the oxen moved at a snail's pace. It was nearly morning before we reached home. But now we had a home. It was our own. There was a wonderful sense of ownership, and the feeling that we were free and did not have to work for others. That feeling bore us through many hardships.

Judge Loren C. Collins was appointed associate justice of the Minnesota Supreme Court in 1880. He was a profound lawyer, an able politician and statesman and one of the leading citizens of his time. The following is written by Collins in "Old Rail Fence Corners":

In 1853, my father visited Eden Prairie. On arriving he found a lynch court in session. A man named Gorman who had squatted upon a very desirable piece of land had gotten into an altercation with a squatter named Samuel Mitchell. These were Irishmen, Gorman a Catholic and Mitchell a Protestant. Gorman had filled Mitchell's left arm full of shot, and the court gave its judgment that Gorman must get out of the country with his family within twenty-four hours. Mr. Gorman had staked out the claim, had built a log house and had ready for crop about two acres of land. My father had $100.00 in gold on him, probably more money than any other man in the community at that time. Gorman sold out to him for the $100.00 and father took possession of the claim.

Father returned to Massachusetts and in the winter we came to Buffalo by rail. In early May we embarked on the steamer Nominee which was then the fastest boat on the river. At the head of the flagstaff was a new broom which indicated that the boat had beaten every other vessel then running on the river north of Galena, Illinois. The captain was Russell Blakely who for many years commanded the best boats belonging to the Packet Company.

We reached St. Paul about ten o'clock on May seventh and I remember very well that the thing which attracted my attention more than any other thing was the newly trimmed cupola of the Territorial Capital Building. There were at least fifteen steamboats at the lower levee when we arrived there, all busy in unloading. They were packed with passengers and freight coming up the river.

Father took a pair of oxen and his wagon from the boat and we made our way up a steep hill from Jackson Street to Third. From there we went up Third to the corner of Wabasha, where father bought some flour and feed. Then we drove back to the boat. About five o'clock in the afternoon the Nominee steamed up the river as far as Fort Snelling, taking at least one-fifth of its passengers and freight. We tied up at the ferry boat landing at the foot of the hill under the old fort, and began to take off our cattle and freight. The hill was very steep leading up to the fort and father, aided by the boys, began to take our goods in small wagon loads to the top of the hill, so we could properly load them. Uncle William, my mother, Aunt Isabel and the small children had been transferred at St. Paul to a small steamboat called the Iola which was to take them up the Minnesota River to Hennepin Landing, a mile or two from our claim in Eden Prairie.

About ten o'clock after we landed at the fort, we started three wagons with a pair of oxen for each and about ten head of cows and young stock. It was a beautiful night with a full moon; and after traveling a mile to what was known as Bloomington Creek, we stopped to graze the cattle and to rest. We all got more or less sleep and it was eight in the morning before we were able to start the cavalcade. We arrived in sight of our future home under most auspicious circumstances. The weather was mild and the sun was shining brightly when we came to a place from where father pointed out the log house at the edge of the woods with a stovepipe through the roof and the smoke coming out. My Uncle Sherbuel had remained an occupant of this house all winter that he might hold this claim of my father's and the one next to it, which had been selected for my Uncle William. Uncle Sherbuel was something of a hunter and trapper, and he had made good use of his time during the winter and had a good assortment of furs; otter, wolf, mink, fox, and those of smaller animals. He had killed several deer and was tanning the hides at the time we arrived. He had also caught and salted several hundred pounds of bass and pickerel.

Father had little money left and we were without seed, except potatoes, for about three acres of our land. Potatoes were of very little value and it was doubtful if it would pay to plant them. But as we had nothing else to put into the ground, father concluded that he would seed the three acres to potatoes. We had a good crop of potatoes and in order to keep them we built a root-cellar out of logs. We dug potatoes and picked them up that fall until I was nearly worn out, but in the spring the demand for potatoes was so great that father sold many bushels at $1.00 a bushel. This gave him a large amount of ready money and he bought a pair of horses.

The next summer my cousin William and I raised a quantity of nice watermelons, the seed having been brought from Springfield, Illinois. In the fall we loaded up two wagons with them and with oxen as the motive power started one afternoon for St. Anthony. We had to make our way down towards Fort Snelling until we came within two miles of the fort. Then we turned toward our destination. It was a long and tedious trip. We camped out over night and did not reach the west bank of the Mississippi River opposite St. Anthony until three o'clock the next afternoon. We fed our cattle in a grove not far from where the Nicollet House now stands, and then we started for the ferry which swung across the Mississippi River about where the stone arch bridge is now. The Island was heavily timbered and the road ran across at an angle, coming out at a bridge on Fifth Street South. We got up onto the street just about the time the men were coming out of the mills, and sold our watermelons and went home with $10.00 each. This was the proceeds of our first farming. It was a three day trip and very tiresome for boys as well as for the cattle.

I had a most tremendous appetite. Our food consisted mostly of potatoes, bread, wheat or corn, beans, and plenty of game. Ducks, chickens or fish could be had by going a few hundred feet in almost any direction. We had no well and all the water we used was hauled from the lake, nearly a half mile distant. Father rigged up a crotch of a tree upon which was placed a water barrel and this was dragged back and forth by a yoke of cattle. Starting from the lake with a full barrel, we had good luck if we reached the house with half of it.

There were plenty of Sioux Indians living in the vicinity of Shakopee. A reddish colored stone about two feet high stood a half mile west of our place on the Indian trail leading from Minnetonka to Shakopee. Around this stone the Indians used to gather, engaged apparently in some religious exercise and smoking kinni kinic.

Iona Raguet of Washington, D.C. presented the history of the Raguet family in Eden Prairie at the Eden Prairie Historical Society meeting December 27, 1971. In 1860, Henry Wynkoop Raguet, with his wife and five children—Condi, Harry, Preston, Margaretta and George—left Zanesville, Ohio for a farm in Eden Prairie. Homer Raguet, son of Preston Raguet, resides on the farm his grandfather purchased in 1859. This farm is on Spring Road in Eden Prairie. Excerpts from My Memoirs by Condi G. Raguet, describe what it was like to be a young boy in Eden Prairie around the 1860s:

The farm in Eden Prairie consisted of 160 acres of prairie land and 80 acres of timberland. When we took the farm over, there were about 50 acres of "broken" land—the term used for cultivated land. My grandfather had paid $1,450 for the farm and at the time of the purchase the broken land had been planted to cereal products—wheat, rye, and oats. Corn was practically unknown in Minnesota at that time.

Our house was on the highest part of the farm and was directly on an Indian trail. From the top of the hill where the house stood, one could look down the valley and see two lakes and the Minnesota River. When we had floods in the spring, as we often did, the lakes and the river were all one body of water covering two miles. Beyond the river, on the other side, the bottom land extended for three miles where another set of bluffs, as hills were called in that country, rose.

We could see both banks of the river from our house, and the bluffs on both sides were high. To the east of this valley were purple prairie lands; on the west the land was covered with heavy timber.

High up on the tablelands ran a little stream, Riley's creek, an outlet of the river, cutting through our land. The surface water that ran into this creek was pure and cold. For many years that was the only water we had on the farm, to drink ourselves and to water the stock. As time went on we at last drilled a well and put up a windmill. Then we had plenty of water without using the creek water. The well water also was pure and cold.

Riley's Lake was about two miles long. It was full of black bass, pickerel and sunfish. The next lake was about a half mile from our house—one of the most beautiful lakes I ever saw. Red Rock, it was called—named after the only boulder I ever saw in Minnesota.

There was another lake, known as Staring Lake. It was long, making a rapid descent from the uplands, and it was surrounded by beautiful timber. It also contained fish, especially wall-eyed pike which, in this part of the country was called jack salmon, as well as many, many sunfish. The lake was overgrown with wild rice. We used to row, troll, skate, and slide on the lakes, in respective seasons.

The first winter we were in Minesota, my father sent me and the hired man named Isaac to get a load of hay. At that time the only hay that was available was cut in the lowlands and was very long. My brother, Harry, tagged along.

Isaac had a six tine fork and I had a three tine fork. I had never used one and didn't know what I was going to do with it.

Isaac said, "I show you how."

When we got on the crest of the bluff, looking down on the meadow onto one of the "rice lakes," as they were called, we saw a group of men, boys, Indians, and children. Isaac, who had been in that part of the country some time knew what it meant.

Said Isaac, "I tank we go fishing." So we went down to the lake and promptly forgot all about the hay. Both whitemen and Indians were engaged in fishing. They were equipped in the same manner as we were—with forks.

It was what we called a "spring hole," about an acre square, an air hole where the fish came up to breathe. We followed the crowd's example and kept at it all day until about 5:00 o'clock. An Indian woman asked me to eat some of the fish, but as they hung the fish upon iron spears over the fire without removing the entrails, I declined. But, the fish were perfectly roasted and in the end I tried them. They were so delicious I ate a great many of them. The mercury was 22 degrees below zero, but with the fire we didn't notice the cold.

Then an incident occurred that Harry and I will remember as long as we live. Harry fell into the spring hole. Strong arms took him out almost immediately, but the water had thoroughly drenched him. The hired man, Isaac, should have taken us to a neighbor's house, but instead he pointed up on the table land and told me to take Harry to Mr. Tirrell's house and that was still some distance away.

Finally we arrived at Mr. Tirrell's house, and Harry, fortunately wasn't frozen. Mrs. Tirrell undressed him, gave him something to eat, put him in a feather bed, and there he slept until Mr. Tirrell saw Isaac and me coming back from the fishing hole to which I had returned after Harry was in good hands.

After Harry had been awakened and dressed, I borrowed some hay and put it all over the hay ladders so that the fish wouldn't fall through. Then we loaded the ladders with the fish and the load was an enormous one.

My father said there were nearly a ton and a half—all black bass, wall-eyed pike and pickerel. We hadn't taken any bullheads or sunfish.

We were told to pack the fish in oats and they would keep indefinitely, for the winters were very cold. We packed them in oats bins until we thought we had enough to last all winter and then took the remainder to St. Paul where we sold them for a good price. I remember the weight was 2,200 pounds, although I don't recall the price. I was too young, at the time, being only twelve and a half years of age, to do the actual selling at the market.

I went to school until I was sixteen, although we only attended school for three months in the winter. During this period I had two excellent teachers to whom I was devoted. I commenced going out with girls before I left Minnesota and danced from the time I was twelve years old.

Our dances were called "country dances" in Minnesota. They were all square dances such as the "munnymusk" and "Virginia Reel." The waltz and other "round" dances had not arrived in Minnesota at that time. We didn't dance the Indian dances.

The neighbors had frequent picnics. Buggies, at that time, were practically unknown in our part of the country. We used to take the girls out in wagons, and the boys who had spring seats in their wagons were in a class by themselves—and knew it. There was only one settler in the township who had a carriage; and he had brought that out from the state of Vermont in 1855.

Esther Moran Hessing of Faribault, Minnesota, presented the history of the Moran family of Eden Prairie at the April 16, 1972, meeting of the Eden Prairie Historical Society:

Our great-grandfather, John N. Moran, was born in Ireland, January 22, 1811. The part of Ireland he was in was made up of Orangemen and he was an ardent one and

Mason jar from the pioneer home of George N. Moran.

remained one until his death. His request was to be buried with orange blossoms on his breast so there would be no question about his loyalties. He graduated from Oxford University with a degree in medicine and spoke many languages. The Ulster-Scots were coming to America and Canada. He followed the crowd and acquired a homestead in Granby, Canada. He was the father of nine children.

My grandfather, George N. Moran, who was the oldest child, came to Minnesota and preempted land on the west side of Mitchell Lake in Eden Prairie in 1854. After settling down he brought his parents, brothers, and sisters here. All of his six children were born in the house he built on this lake. His son, Edwin, remained on the home place. Besides Edwin, the other children were: Alice (Niblett), Harriet (Bear), Ida (Mann), Will, and James. James's son, Everett, and Will's daughter, Mrs. Harry Rogers, still live in Eden Prairie—along with some of their children and grandchildren.

During the Indian uprising, my grandmother made her baby clothes by bending over a Franklin stove—afraid to allow any brighter light to show from the house lest it attract the Indians. The only other means of light at that time were the tallow candles or a

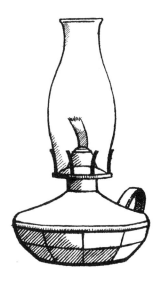

Dwight Picha, son of Abbie Tuckey and Albert Picha, presented the Tuckey family history to the Eden Prairie Historical Society, December 14, 1975:

wick placed in a dish of oil, such as lard. The story has been told many times how proud my grandmother was when her husband, George, bought the first kerosene lamp to arrive in Eden Prairie. They were wary of its safety, for the first kerosene was very explosive, but thankful for the dim light of the small lamp.

An unwritten law of the day assumed the understanding that a traveler who asked for a night's shelter would not be turned away. Two rough looking men stopped one night, but of whom my grandfather was so suspicious that although he allowed them to sleep on the floor, he sat up through the whole night with a gun across his knees.

The Tuckey family originally came from England in the 1600s. The first member of the family to arrive in Eden Prairie was Edson Tuckey. He came in 1869 and purchased land in section 27, known as the Hustad's Creekwood development today. Edson Tuckey was a member of the Volunteer Army of Minnesota during the Civil War before he settled in Eden Prairie.

Edson's brother, Henry, who had served in the army from the state of Massachusetts, came directly to Minnesota after his marriage to Anna Jacobs in Westmillburg, Massachusetts. Grandma Anna recalled that the minister in his prayer asked "to keep them in their journey, far into the land of the setting sun." Minnesota was indeed far away for the girl wife to go from the land of her fathers.

Henry and his wife first settled in Blakely. Anna grew lonesome so they returned to Massachusetts for a visit. Anna's father, Loring Jacobs, returned to Minnesota with them. He brought with him the carpenter tools he had used when he was commissioned to remodel the White House in Washington, D.C. This time the Tuckeys came

Pioneer kitchen in the Henry Tuckey home.

directly to Eden Prairie and purchased land in section 26 by Purgatory Creek on Pioneer Trail. They chose this farm because the contour of the land reminded them of their home in Massachusetts and also it was close to brother Edson's farm.

The Tuckey's lived in the log house on this farm while Anna's father, Loring Jacobs, built the large wood frame house. This house was lived in for almost 100 years until it was purchased and destroyed by the Hustad Realty in 1974.

Eden Mills was located across from the Tuckey home and to meet the needs of the farmers bringing grain to the mill, Henry Tuckey opened a store and post office in the front rooms of the large house. The old ledgers from the Tuckey store show that people bought only basics such as flour, sug-

ar, yeast, kerosene, boots, nails, twine, flypaper and the evil tobacco. One had to pay forty-eight cents for a shirt and a dime for a collar button. Extra services were often performed such as pulling teeth (fifty cents), haircuts (twenty-five cents) and shoeing horses (fifty cents).

The Wolf school was located only one hundred yards from the Tuckey home so it was very available for the students who liked their penny candy. Many of the teachers roomed and boarded with the Tuckeys.

The Presbyterian church was about one-eighth of a mile up the road. For a time one minister served both the Methodist and Presbyterian churches and quite regularly had dinner with the Tuckeys on Sunday. Henry's son, Wallace, would then drive him

The John Goodrich Summer Hotel on Staring Lake. Located on Pioneer Trail. Courtesy of the Hennepin County Historical Society.

to the Dan Patch railroad station in Bloomington for his journey back to Minneapolis.

The long dining room table in the Tuckey home seemed to be always ready for extra guests. Many friends and relatives came each summer to spend a weekend or a week on the farm. The Tuckey place, with its well-kept buildings, spacious lawn and flower gardens, was one of the beauty spots of Eden Prairie.

Mrs. Charles Hulbert talked about the Goodrich, Hulbert and Hankins families in an interview with Clifford Holm for the Hennepin County Historical Society, December 14, 1939.

The Goodrich Family

Horace H. Goodrich owned a hotel and stagecoach route in New Hampshire. The stage coach route was from White Mountain to Mount Washington. Because he housed the draft officers during the Civil War, the populace fired his hotel. It was completely destroyed. As far as it's known he moved with his family directly to the west and located in Eden Prairie in 1867.

Horace Goodrich built a house and a general store on Pioneer Trail about where the Nelson Ryan Flight Headquarters are today. The Staring post office was located in the store. Above the store was the Goodrich Hall. Here, the Grange and other organizations held their meetings. There are memories of the many parties and social functions that also took place in this hall.

Mr. Goodrich's two sons, Fred and John, built large homes across from the store. John operated his home as a summer hotel for a list of distinguished guests. It was famous for its chicken dinners. Officers and their wives from Fort Snelling drove out from the fort for these dinners. Many guests came by train where Mr. Goodrich's man, Joseph, met them at the Eden Prairie station in the "surrey with the fringe on top."

People came for the day, the weekend, and some stayed a week or more. They played lawn games such as croquet in the spacious front yard and went swimming in Staring Lake. Racks of colored canoes lined the beach on Staring Lake.

The house is gone, but the memories of the good times at the Goodrich summer hotel on Staring Lake are kept alive by the people who took the time to write about them.

The Hulbert Family

In 1866, William Frank Hulbert started west from Pittsfield, Michigan, and settled in Eden Prairie. His farm consisted of about 200 acres. When he first arrived with his family the only house available was the log cabin on the farm. Here the family lived until a large frame house was built in 1878.

William Hulbert's son, Charles, grew up in Eden Prairie. He married Loretta Lucy Goodrich in 1891. They had two sons, Karl and Harold. Charles Hulbert was active in the Methodist Church, the Masonic Lodge in Shakopee, the Scottish Rite in Minneapolis and the Modern Woodman of America in Eden Prairie. He served on the Eden Prairie town board and was a member of the Jarrett school board. In 1931, he was elected to the State Legislature where he served for sixteen years. There is a "Hulbert Diary of Yearly Events" beginning in 1900 and concluding with the year 1936.

The Hankins Family

George Valentine Hankins was a hatter by trade in New York. Due to the advent of machinery, George Hankins lost his business. He decided to go west with his two sons, as he was a widower. They arrived in St. Anthony in 1859. Mr. Hankins' son-in-law, Dr. Jarrett Daniels, was an Indian agent with headquarters in Mankato. The Minnesota River was the northern boundary of his territory, so he had located two places for the Hankins family to choose from when they arrived to make their home.

The first place he selected was the King farm, which was located on what is now Lake Street. This farm extended from Lake Street to 36th Avenue South and included what is now Lakewood Cemetery and from Lake Calhoun east to either Lyndale or Nicollet Avenue. This farm was rejected because it was considered too inconvenient to transportation facilities.

The other place was in Eden Prairie and was accepted. It was considered ideally located, being but three miles from Hennepin Landing on the Minnesota River which made transportation to and from Fort Snelling convenient. The fort was also the trading post and took care of all the material needs of the first settlers until they established stores in their own settlements.

The Hankins family arrived by ox team and first stopped at the Jonas Staring home in Eden Prairie. On January 1, 1881, George H. Hankins' son, Alexander, took as his bride Jeannette Ellen Goodrich.

Alexander Hankins operated a feed mill on his farm in the 1880s. He and John Goodrich had the first threshing machine in Eden Prairie. It was operated by horse power. Later, each had their own machine run by a steam engine.

A tribute to Mildred and Martin Grill by Helen H. Anderson, Eden Prairie Historical Society, January, 1971:

(From) The House by the Side of the Road

Let me live in a house by the side of
the road,
    Where the race of men go by—
The men that are good and the men
that are bad,
    As good and as bad as I,
I would not sit in the scorner's seat,
    Or hurl the cynic's ban.
Let me live in a house by the side of
the road
    And be a friend to man.
                    —Sam Walter Ross

George Valentine Hankins.

This is the home of the Martin Grills at 13600 Pioneer Trail in Eden Prairie. Many have walked up the shady lane and found warmth and friendship at the door.

Entering the Grill home by the side door one finds himself in the large kitchen which was the hub of activity on the farm. Along with the modern appliances stands the big black stove, now silent, and the long oak table where the hired help received three good meals a day. In one corner is the big roll-top desk where all business transactions took place. To the side of the room is the stairway leading up to the hired men's quarters.

Open a door, take one step and one enters the private life of Mildred and Martin Grill. This room should be called the friendship room as it seems everything in it is associated with a friend. The oil paintings on the walls were painted by a clergyman friend, who as a young college student came asking for a summer job. He not only got a job, but the support he needed to achieve his goal in the Christian ministry. Many of the painted plates and the pieces in her cut glass collections are gifts from family and friends. The next room, without a doubt, was called the parlor in days gone by. Here stands the music cabinet, the Chickering grand piano and

The log cabin home of Mr. and Mrs. John R. Cummins.

John R. Cummins built this house with lumber from the butternut trees that grew on his farm. Bricks were hauled from the Chaska Brick Works by horse and wagon in 1879.

33

John R. Cummins with a bowl of apples from his experimental orchard. Paintings by his wife, Martha Clark Cummins, on the wall.

the Baldwin organ. This is Mildred's room. Many little girls in Eden Prairie took their first music lessons from Mildred. She was always willing to play for the church services in both the Methodist and Presbyterian churches. For many years she was the organist for her Eastern Star chapter in Hopkins. Sitting in this room for a few minutes one gets the feeling this yellow brick house that was built over a hundred years ago has a story to tell. In brief, this is it:

Simon Schearer secured the land by preemption and Entry No. 33 on October 13, 1855. J. R. Cummins bought the land from Mr. Schearer in 1856. A little log house in a grove of butternut trees was the Cummins home while Mr. Cummins cut down the butternut trees and sawed them into lumber for the big brick house he built across the road from the cabin. The bricks for the exterior of the house were hand-made in Chaska and hauled by wagon to the farm.

Mr. Cummins spent his leisure hours making hand-carved furniture out of butternut wood taken from his farm. Mrs. Cummins painted scenes of the beautiful prairie. Mr. Cummins was a horticulturist of note in the area, experimenting with apples and grapes in an attempt to find varieties that could withstand the cold Minnesota winters.

In 1908, Edwin and Harriet Phipps, Mildred's parents, bought the farm plus nearby land which increased the size of the farm to about 385 acres. A great share of this farm is now part of the Flying Cloud Airport.

Mr. Phipps was a vegetable gardener from north Minneapolis. His specialty was asparagus. He was known as the "Asparagus King of Hennepin County."

Martha Clark Cummins in her parlor.

Harriet Phipps had been a teacher of languages in the Minneapolis schools. She was also a graduate of the S.S. Curry School of Expression in Boston. Naturally she was called upon to direct the plays and programs in the community, often adding bits of her own prose and poetry. She loved flowers. The yard was ablaze with blooms in the summer and fall. Her greatest joy and pride was the peony bed with its 400 or more plants. Folks who attended the Presbyterian and Methodist churches looked forward to peony time for then Mrs. Phipps would bring tubs of peonies to each church. Just think how much the beauty and fragrance of those peonies added to the worship service on a Sunday in June.

Mrs. Phipps liked to express her appreciation for the bounties of nature and the love of the farm in bits of poetry such as this:

Farm Joys

On a summer morning, over on the
   farm,
Getting early breakfast has a won-
   drous charm,
Hear the fire crackle, hear the kettle
   sing,
Smell the coffee steaming, best of
   everything,
Bacon sizzling in the pan, wheat
   cakes light and brown,
Never ate a better meal anywhere in
   town.
Now the sun comes stealing through
   the early dawn,
And the wild birds' twitter ushers in
   the morn,
Mr. Rooster's lusty crow echoes loud
   and clear,
Telling all his farm yard friends that
   the day is here.

Besides the things I've mentioned, I
find the greatest charm
Sitting at early breakfast with home
folks on the farm.

The Farmer's Life

"Saw ye the farmer at his plow,
As you were riding by,
Or wearied 'neath the noonday heat,
When summer suns were high?
And thought you that his lot was
hard,
And did you thank your God,
That you and yours were not
condemned
Thus like a slave to plod?"

"Come see him at his harvest home,
His heart felt pleasures see,
And you may better judge how
blessed
The farmer's life may be."

Forsaken

I watch each day at the window,
I listen each night at the door,
For the sound of the gentle footsteps
Perhaps I may hear no more.
A vision is ever before me,
Of a sweet and gentle face,
Brown eyes and curling locks,
And a form of fairy grace.
She left us in the springtime,
With never a tear or sigh;
I wait alone for her coming,
As the weary days go by.
I am lonely and forsaken,
And, as the days roll on,
I ask myself over and over again,
"Where has my little dog gone?"

On December 13, 1975, Martin Grill gave up his earthly journey. The next year the City of Eden Prairie bought the farm for a community park with the stipulation that Mildred could live out her life in the house where she had lived all her life, among the things dear to her and her memories.

The Eden Prairie Historical Society honored the four Miller brothers—Arthur, Frederick, Norman and Harold—and their cousin, Emil Pauly, at the March 12, 1972, meeting. Children, grandchildren and many friends were in attendance. Following are notes from a recorded interview with Arthur Miller, on January 24, 1971, by Mrs. Rolland Doughty and Mrs. Calvin Anderson:

My mother's dad, William Lenzen, came from Koblenz, Germany. People were leaving Germany to avoid going into the army only to come here and become involved in the Civil War. The Lenzens first moved into Ohio. A family by the name of Keyes came from the same area in Germany. Grandpa married one of the Keyes girls. They came west in 1850 and Grandpa preempted a farm in Eden Prairie. It was located northwest of Hwy. 5 and County Rd. 4 where the Prairie Village Mall is to be located someday.

The name Miller was spelled Muller in Germany. The name Fredrick spans five generations in the Miller family.

Grandpa Fred Miller was married in Chicago to Charlotte Mathies. He came to Minnesota and bought a farm southwest of Riley Lake. My great-grandfather died in 1860 on this farm from black diptheria and was buried right on this farm. When this farm was sold they did not move his grave because of this contagious disease. His grave is still there. Grandpa bought a farm west of Chanhassen on County Road 41 and Highway 5. This was later sold and he bought the Samuel Mitchell farm in Eden Prairie. Sam Mitchell had preempted this land in 1853. Grandpa died when my dad was fifteen and a half years old. Dad stayed on this farm with his mother and sisters until he was nineteen years old. He then started on his own and bought the Rankin store north of the railroad tracks on County Road 4 in Eden Prairie. The Rankin store was the location of the Washburn post office. Mr. Rankins was the postmaster. Dad took his brother, John, into the business.

The Fred F. Miller family. Back row: Fred, Jr., Arthur, Harold. Front row: Katherine Miller, Norman, Fred F. Miller.

They bought the land south of the tracks from Rankins and had Jim Clark build a store and house. This store, our house, and grandmother Miller's house burned December 5, 1963. Dad married Katherine Lenzen. Brother John married Mary Lenzen, and Henry Pauly married Christine Lenzen.

Nick Pauly, grandfather of Emil, and his three brothers came from Luxembourg to this area in 1850. Nick Pauly settled near Lake Susan south of Chanhassen where the Lyman turkey farm is today. At this time Highway 101 was the old Indian trail from Shakopee. Henry Pauly was born in 1855 and was the first white child to be born in Carver County. He married Christine Lenzen of Eden Prairie. He bought land next to the Lenzen place. Here, Emil and his three brothers were born. Later, Emil operated this farm. He raised his six children here and his youngest son, Roger, is now living on the home place.

You could find most anything you might want in our old Miller Brothers store—groceries, clothing, patent medicines, even poisons. Dad would go to Chaska for a side of beef, cut it up, and sell T-bones for twenty-five cents a pound.

A blacksmith shop was built about 1880. A Mr. Bladdle was the blacksmith. He lived right in his shop. Farmers came here to get their wheels set and their horses shod.

In 1902, the Miller brothers built an elevator. They bought grain from the farmers and hauled it into the Minneapolis Grain Exchange.

There was a creamery across from the store. It was built in 1884. This creamery burned and a much better one was built. Soon milk routes were formed. Some of the early milk haulers were Rubin Jarrett, John Rogers, John Brown, John Nesbitt, Emil Pauly, Charles Hulbert and Mr. Blakeborough. The milk was taken to a number of creameries in the city. I remember the Rice Creamery. When the Twin City Milk Producers Association was organized in 1916 the milk routes were taken over by this association. The Eden Prairie Creamery closed and was auctioned off. Fred Miller got it. He sold the equipment and used the lumber to build a house for his son, Fred.

Dad used to get up about one or two o'clock in the morning and drive to town with a load of butter and eggs. He'd return late at night with a wagon full of groceries. One night a train hit his wagon when he got near home. The horses ran as far as the old Methodist church. There was a lawsuit and the railroad paid for the groceries.

The first telephone in Eden Prairie was installed in the Miller Brothers store by the

37

Northwestern Telephone Co. of Minneapolis. This was a free phone. The telephone company did not charge us for the use of it. Everyone in town used the phone. Messages were relayed throughout the town by the use of this phone. Soon other companies started installing phones. A line from Shakopee took care of most of the homes. The Tri-State came from Jordan and served the southwestern part of the town. The phones cost one dollar a month and many paid their bill once a year. There were twelve to fourteen on a line. Each home had its own ring. When the phone rang and one lifted the receiver often he would hear a click, click, click. This let you know everyone was listening to your conversation. Around 1946 the Bell Telephone took over the Shakopee and Tri-State lines.

First the kerosene lamps furnished our light. Dad then had a gasoline machine that piped gas for lights in the house, store and hall. Around 1909, John McQueen, John Rogers (he lived on the Douglas place) and the Millers put in the first electricity. It cost $1,000. McQueen paid $500 and the Rogers and Millers each paid $250. Soon Hulberts, Jarretts and others along the road connected up. A number of farms had their own electric plants run by gasoline engines. A co-op electric from Jordan took care of the Riley Lake and river bluff area.

Dad furnished kerosene for his customers. When the gas engine came in he put in a two-hundred-gallon tank. We got our gas in five-gallon cans from Excelsior and put it in the big tank. We sold it by the gallon. Dad had the first gas tank in Eden Prairie. I think it's still standing.

The hall above the store served as the village hall before the consolidated school was built. All gatherings took place in this hall —elections, milk meetings, dances, medicine shows, etc. The dances were great fun. An orchestra was hired and we'd usually have around seven sets of square dancers. We'd dance until two or three in the morning. The American Legion used to give dances up there. After I came home from

the service there was a dance up there and the old building was swaying like an accordion. I told Dad they'd have to stop or we'll all be down in the basement. From then on, just wedding dances were held in the hall. I remember Emil Pauly had his wedding dance up there. We had many good times around this old town in those days.

I remember the Woodman of America held their meetings up there. I remember Mother fixing the oysters for their annual oyster dinner on her kitchen range and carrying it upstairs. One time there was a medicine show up in the hall. A train was parked on the main track. It was doing some switching. Another train came from Chaska and banged into this train and knocked the bell off the train and blew a hole in the boiler. Steam shot way over to the store. You should have seen the people scram out of that hall. The stove in the caboose started a fire. Produce was scattered over the track.

Dr. Smith from Shakopee was the first doctor to serve this area. Then came Dr. Fisher and Dr. Buck. One time Dr. Smith picked me up on my way home from school in Chanhassen. How proud I felt riding in his 1908 model car.

We boys had a little cabin near Mitchell Lake. We moved this cabin to an island on Red Rock Lake. We bought logs from Ezra Paine and floated them over to the island. A bigger cabin was built. Here we had fun fishing in the summer and trapping in the winter.

When deer season came, Dad didn't care if school kept or not. He'd go up north and sometimes stay for a month. At this time each hunter could take home five deer. The men would take the train up to Grand Rapids, Minnesota. They'd hire a team and drive forty miles out to some logging camp. The men shipped the deer home by train. One time Dad got into a camp where there was lice. I remember him coming home and Mom not letting him in the house until he got rid of the lice.

Harry Rogers' daughter, Phyllis Rogers Kopesky, presented the Rogers family history to the Eden Prairie Historical Society on April 13, 1975. The Fellowship Hall of the Eden Prairie Presbyterian Church, where the meeting was held, was filled to capacity with Rogers family members: sons and daughters down to great great-grandchildren of John Rogers.

John Rogers was born on March 24, 1873, in Castle Morton Parish, Worcestershire, England. He came to the United States in 1892 and on to Eden Prairie in 1897.

The first stop in Eden Prairie was the Schmidel farm, which is now the Glenrose Floral greenhouse. He inquired about employment and the Schmidels sent him to Charles Hulbert. While working for Mr. Hulbert, he rented small pieces of land around Eden Prairie. One piece of land was on the Minnesota River bottoms at Shakopee. Near his land was an Indian camp and he hired the Indians to help him with his celery that was his largest crop. When he needed supplies, he traveled by canoe with the Indians to Shakopee and back.

For a time the Rogers family lived in the Douglas house near the Eden Prairie station. One of the advantages of living there was that they were one of the first three homes in Eden Prairie to have electricity. Here their four children—Roland, Harry, Helen and Alice—spent their childhood. John later moved to a farm on Pioneer Trail.

At this time the products raised in Eden Prairie were sent to the Minneapolis markets by rail or with horses and wagon. John and Joseph Pemberton started the earliest horse-drawn milk route from Eden Prairie to Minneapolis. Later, John operated one of the first truck milk routes.

John Rogers bought cattle and shipped them to St. Paul by rail to the stockyards. He convinced the Minneapolis-St. Louis Railroad to build a corral and loading chute near the Eden Prairie Depot. Many neighboring farmers also used this corral and chute. Later, he bought and sold cattle that he transported to South St. Paul by truck.

John Rogers was interested in community affairs. He was a member of the school board for twenty years and a member of the town board for twenty-five years, serving part of this time as chairman.

John Rogers persuaded other members of his family to come to the states. The only one who settled and lived in Eden Prairie all his life was a nephew, James, father of Donald, Arthur and Richard of Eden Prairie.

John Rogers continued to be active in farming at his home on Pioneer Trail until eighteen days before his eighty-sixth birthday. At the time of his death he had fifteen grandchildren, fifty-four great-grandchildren and six great great-grandchildren.

From the Minneapolis Star, January 1, 1945, an interview with William Anderson on his eighty-eighth birthday:

Looking back over my other birthdays, I think the happiest ones were those spent in the pleasures of pioneer life in Eden Prairie. Folks really enjoyed themselves back in those days. They were the days of big families, good neighbors and real friends.

The only means of transportation was homemade sleds drawn by ox teams, which also plowed the fields. On these sleds we loaded our families to take them to church or parties at the neighbors. On Christmas and other holidays we had big celebrations and the event of the day was a "sheep shoot" with sheep as prizes.

It was a day's journey to town but we were always rewarded by a visit to the refreshment barrel which merchants always kept open in the basement.

I was one of three school board members when there were only seven children attending the Anderson school. In 1880, I was elected to the state legislature and served

State Representative William Anderson begins the long drive to St. Paul in the 1880's.

for a number of years. I was proud to serve our area for it was a settlement that stood for integrity, industry and high ideals.

(Because William Anderson was not of age when he came to Eden Prairie, his farm was preempted by his mother, Elizabeth Anderson. From 1940 to 1960, the land was owned by Truman J. Beggs, a great-grandson of Elizabeth Anderson. It is now the location of the Minnesota Protective Life Insurance Company building.)

The following was written by Robert Anderson, about 1890, found in the Anderson family papers:

During the first few years of settlement in this town, matters were unsettled and unsatisfactory in condition. Little regard was paid to observance of the Sabbath—working Sundays, hunting, fishing, claim hunting, jumping of claims, brawls, quarrels over claims and boundary lines, and several shootings took place. But, as things settled down, many good people founded schools and churches. They sowed the seed that has been watered and nurtured by their children who followed in their footsteps. These first pioneers lived, died, and were buried, but their influence was not buried with them. It lived on.

I'd like to mention something about the first young people who grew up in the log cabins of Eden Prairie. There was Judge Loren Collins, a self-made man. He studied law. He became one of the Supreme Court Judges of the State of Minnesota. He, also, was Division Commander of the Grand Army of the Republic and would undoubtably have been Governor of the State of Minnesota had he not been cheated out of the nomination through political trickery.

Robert Anderson

40

Another of our dear pioneer boys, Captain C.B. Tirrell, studied law, was admitted to the bar, enlisted in the army, was made captain in his company and afterwards elected a member of the State Legislature.

Two more boys were admitted to the bar as lawyers—Mr. Stacy in Arizona and Mr. Lucas, now practicing in Minneapolis. Seven other young men were doctors, two were dentists. Four of our bright young men have taught in higher halls of learning. One is a professor at Stanford University and another is teaching and lecturing in Syracuse, New York. Seventeen more of our young men have entered business for themselves and are successful business men. Thirteen more of our young men hold positions of responsibility with credit to themselves and satisfaction to their employers.

I need scarcely say anything about the brave boys who have remained on the farms. Sufficient to say, they are filling their calling nobly, giving their young folk a good chance to get an education, supporting the church, and helping to furnish the bread and butter that feeds the world.

The Czech Settlement in Eden Prairie

In the years immediately following the unsuccessful revolution of 1848, the Czechs in the mountainous districts of Bohemia and Moravia were finding life more and more unbearable. They were irked by political oppression; the economic status of the majority was deplorable; many chafed under the requirements imposed by military service and under the religious intolerance of the government. At the beginning of the 1850s the United States immigration agents found fertile soil for propaganda among these unhappy people.

Wisconsin was then making efforts to attract settlers from northern and central Europe. Germans were immigrating to the vicinity of Milwaukee, where they were joined by large groups of Czechs who were familiar with their language.

Many of the Czechs selected the towns of Racine and Caladonia as their first destination upon arrival in the United States. The report of free land farther west lured many on. Some settled in an area later known as Silver Lake. But the largest settlement was in the Minnetonka-Hopkins area and among the hills of northern Eden Prairie. At the close of the Civil War there were 120 families in this area. On the Hennepin County map of 1879, which gives the names of land owners, the following Bohemian names are found in Eden Prairie: Smetana, Picha, Kopesky, Kuchera, Bren, Kurtz, Cherveny, Holasek and Plehal.

In this new land the Czechs made an effort to live among those they had known in the old country. They clung together, speaking their own language and preserving their national customs and traditions. They helped each other clear land and build homes in the wilderness. They worked hard and gradually built up good farms and raised families who were a credit to the community.

The Biography of Grandpa Kucera

Grandpa Kucera's biography was written in Czech and translated by Olga Bren of Hopkins. Margaret Picha Bren (Mrs. John Bren) gave a copy to the Eden Prairie Historical Society. Space will not permit telling the life of Mr. Kucera in northern Bohemia. But times were hard and so around 1865 he and his wife decided to take their three children—Anna, Pepina and Josef—and go to America. Grandpa Tesarek, Mrs. Kucera's father, came with them. The biography follows:

We put ourselves into God's hands and into his care and started over the great ocean to a strange land where we didn't even have a friend; but, standing firm in the hope that there things would be better and that we could buy land for our children. God gave us those hopes about which we thought and hoped for in Europe.

So we bought land, forty acres by a lake (Duck Lake). We began building and farming and working hard. God blessed us in our work. Some people noticed this and said to us, "Your children will have it good because you are providing for them a good beginning." God prospered us and we saw that our children had it good. We now have seven children—four boys. Each wanted eighty acres of land so we took care of that.

There is something I want to tell you about our trip here. We got to St. Paul and now we had hard times. We had to talk and no one could understand us to tell us where to go. I told people "Minnetonka" and they would shake their heads. They didn't know what I meant and they would answer, "He, he." So I told Mama to sit in the depot as I was to go part way up the street to look for some Czechs. So I went. It was near evening and there were many people walking. I kept asking, "Are you Czech?" and they would answer, 'He." There were two men sitting on a bench. I went to them and asked,"Are you Czech?" and they answered, "We are Czech." They were Frank Kinsel and Vaclav Dostel. I was glad to see them. They were from the place I wanted to go. They told me everything and I went back to the depot to tell Mama.

So in the morning, I set out with Grandpa for "Minnetonka" to Brens, the same way the boys told us to go. They said Bren would go for the trunk and Mama in St. Paul. When we came where the roads separated by Burns by the school (east Hopkins), the sign showed road to "Minnetonka" so we followed it. But we should have gone straight a little farther and asked Millers about the Empanger house and we would have been among the Czechs. It started to sprinkle so we hurried more and soon came to "Minnetonka."

I went into a house and started talking Czech and again they said, "He." It was evening and we wanted a night's lodging. They understood that. They gave us eat and found a neighbor who talked Czech so we got to Brens. Bren sent Joseph to the depot for Mama, the children and the trunk; and so we all cried. It took us four days to come from St. Paul to Brens. It was Saturday before Svatim Duchem (Holy Ghost Day) in 1868. We stayed in a corn crib for eight weeks and then bought forty acres of land. Winter was on our necks. We had $530. I paid $350 for the land, $80 for the house, $33 for a stove and $45 for a cow. We bought flour, some dishes, shoes, and the money was gone. There was a wood around our house so the wind didn't bother us.

We started farming for our livelihood. We had our own field and that made us happy. After a few years, we bought eighty acres with which was a lake. So we farmed and built and the children helped. Times were very hard. We had debts, but we also had some money. But we had a start and we took advantage of it and with God's help we accomplished what we started out to accomplish.

America was worthwhile for us for which we all thank God so we wouldn't be like the hogs who feed on acorns but never look up to see where the acorns fall from. Finally, my dear children, I am begging you to not forget our good fortune and take care of your inheritance which you got with our help. May God bless you. Keep the sabbath all day in honor of God. Read the Bible to all children. May God advise and lead us that we might meet in our eternal rest.

Written by Joseph F. Kucera in 1914
Your Father

Nell Schmeidel Nesbitt, daughter of William Schmeidel, presented the Schmeidel family history to the Eden Prairie Historical Society November 12, 1971.

The Schmeidel family came from Brandeis, Bohemia to this country in 1853. They settled in Racine and Brinkman's Ridge, Wisconsin. The Soubas, Dominicks, Holaseks and Chasteks came about the same time.

Horace F. Goodrich

George Moran

Robert Glenn

Andrew Glenn

James Gamble

William J. Jarrett

William Nesbitt

James Anderson

Eden Prairie Pioneers.

Joseph Schmeidel married Rosalia Souba in 1857. Joseph was a mason by trade. Rosalia used to help her husband in his trade, carrying the heavy bricks to wherever he was laying them. They are thought to have had sixteen children.

Joseph's wife, Rosalia, learned the art of caring for a large family. She made soap, candles, butter, pumpkin-butter, using the big black kettle that all pioneer families had. She dried apples and other fruits. She saved seeds from her vegetables for planting the following year. She did all the family sewing, making even the suits for her boys and husband using the painstaking back-stitch, since there was no sewing machine. She was a midwife and helped all her neighbors. She knew medicinal plants and gathered roots, barks, leaves, berries, and knew how to use them successfully.

The Joseph Schmeidels moved to a farm near the Glen Lake Sanitarium in 1868. They were true pioneers, sharing work with their neighbors in times of building barns, homes, and when harvesting crops.

Joseph Schmeidel had a sermon book in Czech and conducted prayer meetings in his home. The Plihal, Holaseks, Brens, and others came to these meetings. How they needed this spiritual fellowship and these meetings provided it. It was these groups that were active in the organization of the John Hus Presbyterian Church at Deephaven Junction, now Faith Presbyterian Church. Joseph often led the meetings at the church when there wasn't a minister present.

My Father, William Schmeidel, lived on a farm east of Riley's Lake. Our house was a big nine-room brick structure with fine oak, maple, and butternut trees all around. He planted a big apple orchard and harvested many bushels of fine wealthies, hybernals, duchess and crab apples which he sold in the Minneapolis markets. Father loved the soil and was a master farmer, taking pride in his fields, the orchard he planted and his home. I can still see him sitting on his porch on a rainy day enjoying the refreshing drops as they came to water the thirsty earth. Father took an active part in the Methodist Church and served on the church board. He also served on the school board and the town board. Life was good with Father and Mother on the farm.

Dean Holasek, son of Mr. and Mrs. Alvin Holasek, gave the Holasek family history for the Eden Prairie Historical Society on April 8, 1973, during a reunion of the Holasek families.

Joseph Holasek, with his wife and two-year-old daughter, Anna, came from Bohemia in 1854, sailing across the Atlantic to the St. Lawrence River. At Quebec they took a small steamboat down the St. Lawrence River to the Great Lakes. They crossed the Great Lakes to a Bohemian settlement at Racine, Wisconsin. Coming over at the same time were Mrs. Holasek's parents and young brother, the Chastek family. The Chasteks stayed in Racine for two years, then followed to Minnesota. The Holaseks went from Racine to Chicago by train and then across country to Galena, Illinois. From here they took a steamboat up the Mississippi River to Fort Snelling.

At Fort Snelling they were directed to a Bohemian settlement just starting up west of Minneapolis.

The Holaseks built a temporary log cabin on the southwest shore of Shady Oak Lake and lived there while Joseph scouted around for farm land. In 1857 he bought the first land on Bryant Lake. He picked this land because it was on a lake and had a creek flowing through it. There were also several springs on it. They built their first log cabin on the creek beside one of the springs. As the family grew larger, a big cabin was built in a clearing where the present house stands. The Holaseks had a family of fourteen children. Two of them died in infancy. As there were no churches or cemeteries,

Holasek Homestead, 1917.

the two were buried on the hill overlooking the lake just west of the homestead. Mrs. Holasek's father was also buried there. Alvin, a grandson, remembers Grandma Holasek taking him out to see the graves on the hill showing him the stones which were just field stones with no inscription on them.

Grandpa Holasek worked hard and was always quick to take advantage of an opportunity. He saw he could pick wild fruit and take it into Minneapolis where it sold quickly as there was no fruit to be had. Some years there were large crops of cranberries on the marshes. These sold especially well as the city grew larger.

Mr. Holasek picked out the best wild plums he could find and kept planting them till he had several acres around the house. As they came into bearing, he thinned them out, keeping those with the biggest and best fruit. Soon, he was hauling plums to Minneapolis by the wagon load. He was not too

successful with apples but he did get hold of some tame grape plants. Soon, there were grapes to sell and plenty of grape wine to treat anyone who stopped in.

Annie, the oldest daughter who was born in Bohemia, married Frank Kinsel. Her father provided her with a farm on the north shore of Glen Lake. The Kinsels donated land on the northwest corner of their farm on Excelsior Blvd. for a Bohemian hall. This was operated by the Z.C.B.J., a Bohemian fraternal brotherhood. Their meetings were held on Sunday afternoon after which they often had a dance. On the Fourth of July they always had a big celebration there. The Sokols, with their gymnastic teams, would give an exhibition followed by a dance. (The Sokol organization was formed in Bohemia when the people were subjugated by another nation and were not allowed to have an army or any kind of military training. The people started the Sokol gymnastic team to be in good physical training should the opportunity come to overthrow their conquerors.) They always had a big crowd. Often a group of young people from south Eden Prairie would come and bring Niggermunn with them. He would always dance a jig for them. The street car line soon ran just south of the hall and many people from Hopkins would ride out for the celebration.

Joseph Holasek's daughter, Rose, married Frank Miller, who opened the Rowland General Store on Willow Creek (present home of C.L. Sutton, 7170 Flying Cloud Drive). He built a blacksmith shop across the creek from the store. He then got the Rowland post office established in his store. Before that, the people in northeast Eden Prairie had to go to Edina Mills for their mail. The people in the neighborhood would change off getting the mail. One would take a bag of wheat or corn, throw it over his shoulder and hike to Edina Mills to have it ground and bring back the mail.

Mr. Miller did a good business at the store, selling buggies, wagons, farm machinery and tools. He also carried a big stock of groceries and general merchandise. He even had a big keg standing in the corner back of the potbelly stove so the fellows could play cards and drink hard cider. He bought two threshing rigs from the Minneapolis threshing works in Hopkins. John Bren, Jack Bren's dad, operated one of the rigs covering the territory east of Rowland to Bush Lake, Cahill and Bloomington. His brother-in-law, Emil Holasek, operated the other rig in western Eden Prairie and Chanhassen.

Joseph Holasek's son, Emil, took over the operation of the home farm on the north side of Bryant Lake. He had his own threshing machine for a time, then he started hauling milk. He bought a draft horse stallion and bred a lot of mares for the farmers in this area. He needed horses for himself for hauling milk and then there was a lot of road work close by and he put his teams on the roads. More room was needed for his horses so he built a big addition to his horse barn. As soon as this was finished, there

were barn dances every Saturday night. The Rousher brothers furnished the music. There was always a big keg of beer for the adults and strawberry pop for the children.

Emil Holasek had four children. Two lived in Eden Prairie—Alvin and Fred. Alvin stayed on the home place and operated Rock Isle Park on the north end of the lake. Fred farmed the land on the southwest side of the lake and ran the Holasek's picnic and swimming area on the lake. Super Valu purchased this land for its regional office building headquarters in 1978. The city of Eden Prairie purchased the Alvin Holasek property for a city park. Young people who lived in Eden Prairie in the 1940s and '50s have pleasant memories of the good times swimming at Holaseks on Bryant Lake.

When Grandpa Joseph Holasek passed away in 1880 he had provided farms for ten of his fourteen children. Grandma Holasek stayed on the home farm. She often told her grandson, Alvin, about how glad she was that they had come to America. Over in Bohemia practically all the land belonged to the wealthy nobles. They could not even cut a piece of wood, nor were they allowd to hunt or fish. In this new land there was so much of everything, so much wood for fuel and for building houses and barns. It was so easy to better oneself here.

David LeRoy Pavelka, son of Mr. and Mrs. Melvin Pavelka of Eden Prairie, presented a paper on the "Descendants of Frank Pavelka (1825-1900) and Mary Bren Pavelka (1830-1902)" to the Eden Prairie Historical Society on February 13, 1977. It was a genealogical study encompassing the years 1825 to 1977 with special emphasis on the residents of Hennepin County—especially the communities of Eden Prairie, Edina, Minnetonka and Hopkins.

Frank Pavelka left Bohemia about 1850. He made the long transatlantic voyage and the Great Lakes navigation to the Bohemian settlement near Racine, Wisconsin. At that time Racine was a staging point for western bound settlers and a Czech community had sprung up here. It was in Racine, in the mid 1850s, that Frank met and married Mary Bren, who had also come from Bohemia.

The story of the Pavelkas takes them to Chatfield, Minnesota, then to the Nebraska territory after the passing of the federal Homestead Act of 1862. They had six children.

Their son, John Edward, left home at the age of sixteen. He first went west where he became a cowboy. He learned an Indian dialect and traveled for a time with a wild west show. The late 1870s found him in the Hopkins area, probably visiting his uncles, Frank and Joseph Bren. He worked for Joseph Makousky as a farm hand and at the age of twenty married Joseph Makousky's daughter, Mary. In the early 1900s he settled on land flanking County Road 18. A portion of this land was sold to Joseph Viska, who built a large brick house which is now the home of the Eden Prairie Historical and Cultural Commission.

John Edward Pavelka's son, George Willis, bought forty acres of land in northwest Eden Prairie. He built his house in two phases, the first in 1908 and the second in 1912. His son, Melvin, now lives on this place and the house is still there. It is the office for Countryside Auto Parts, a business operated by Melvin Pavelka and his son, David.

George Pavelka died in 1955 in the house he had built for his family. He was buried in the cemetery adjacent to the John Hus Presbyterian Church (now Faith Presbyterian Church), the church and cemetery built by the first Bohemian pioneers in this area.

The following account of the Joseph Bren family was written by a grandson, John Bren, and given to the Eden Prairie Historical Society in 1979:

Joseph and Emilie Bren came from Svate Katre'awa, Moravia in 1881. Letters from relatives in the Hopkins-Minnetonka area told of the rich land and opportunities for a better life in Hennepin County, Minnesota. This influenced them to take off for the new land across the big ocean with their four small children. Adolph, who was about three years old, had smallpox on the ship.

When my grandparents arrived in this area they were met by the Cherveny family who encouraged them to stay at their home. My grandfather had only $7.00 left in his pocket. Both Grandpa and Grandma soon found work at the Bryant and Holasek farms. Grandma washed clothes for the Bryants and also helped Grandpa cut trees and make hay. The land had many trees that had to be cleared before the land could be used for farming. They carried the heavy logs out of the woods on their shoulders. The hay they cut was carried out of the meadows on long poles that were pushed under the piles of hay. Most of the wood and hay was hauled to Minneapolis and sold.

Mr. Bryant sold my grandparents their first eighty acres and offered to build them a house which was built by Winslow Dvorak for $40.00. This house has been remodeled several times and is still occupied. The farm was bounded by Bryant Lake, Highway 169 and the Crosstown.

Over the years the family grew to thirteen children. As soon as the children reached working age they worked for other farmers, usually making hay and cutting wood.

There was a good market for fruits and vegetables in Minneapolis. As the hilly land was best suited for raising fruits and vegetables, these became their main crops. They did have a few cows and sold milk. When the sons started farming they raised strawberries and raspberries. They hired berry pickers from Silver Lake, Minnesota and boarded them for the season. Frank and John both married girls who had picked berries.

The Brens lived next to Bryant Lake and spent as much times as work permitted for swimming and fishing. A little extra money was taken in by renting boats to fishermen.

All the Brens were religious people and helped organize the first Czech Protestant church near Hopkins, now Faith Presbyterian Church. Before the church was built in 1887, the people met in the homes and worshipped together. Many of the people in the area found it difficult to get to church during the busy seasons of the year for it was some distance away, so a little Sunday School building was built on my grandfather's farm. He donated the land which went back to him when new means of transportation made it easier to get to the big church.

The sons of Joseph and Emilie Bren all bought farms next to one another. The daughters married neighboring farmers. An interesting fact is that most of the Brens married someone from the neighborhood and only two didn't marry Czechs. These families all lived within a mile from each other. The last of the original Bren farm was sold to the City of Eden Prairie in 1978 for a community park.

OUR COMMUNITY

TOWNSHIP OF EDEN PRAIRIE
1858-1962

Land Survey

On May 20, 1785, the Continental Congress adopted the plan of dividing public lands into six-mile-square townships with each township divided into thirty-six sections, the measurements running from established meridians and base lines, or parallels. Sections sixteen and thirty-six were to be designated as state school lands.

As soon as public lands were surveyed they were opened for preemption, or sale, by a proclamation of the President. In the Minnesota Territory, the land east of the Mississippi River was surveyed and opened for preemption in 1849, the land west of the river in 1855. Preempted land sold for $1.25 an acre. The state school lands, sold in 1862, brought a higher price of five dollars to ten dollars an acre. All the land in Eden Prairie was surveyed and preempted by 1855.

Hennepin County

On March 6, 1852, the territorial legislature passed an act which established Hennepin County and contained provisions for its organization and government. The first meeting of the county board was October 21, 1852, and consisted of three members elected at large.

Before the townships were organized for local government purposes the county assessors, justices of peace and constables were appointed by the territorial government. For Eden Prairie, Hiram Abbott was appointed justice of the peace and William O. Collins was appointed constable.

In 1858, the new state legislature provided that the business of Hennepin County government should be conducted by a board of men consisting of the chairmen of the boards of supervisors of all the townships in the county, together with a number of men from the villages of St. Anthony and Minneapolis. This made a board of twenty to thirty members.

Some difficulty arose in the organization of this first large board. In examining credentials, many present could not prove evidence of election or appointment. While the chairman of every board was an ex-officio member of the county board, some did not avail themselves of the privilege of sitting on the board. Probably one reason townships were not represented was because of the long distances to travel when it was slow to go by team or horseback and still more difficult by walking. Aaron Gould represented Eden Prairie on this first board.

This county board was discontinued after a two-year trial. The county was then divided into five districts with five elected commissioners. Today there is a seven-member county board.

Eden Prairie Town Board

A brief history of Eden Prairie, found in Dr. Edward D. Neill's "History of Hennepin County," states that the township held its first meeting in the little Gould log schoolhouse on May 11, 1858, the same day Minnesota became a state. The following officers were elected:

Supervisors	Aaron Gould, chairman
	Robert Anderson
	William O. Collins
Clerk	William H. Rouse
Collector	A.K. Miller
Assessor	William J. Jarrett
Overseer of the Poor	John Kelly
Justice of the Peace	William O. Collins
	James Gamble
Constables	A.K. Miller
	Archie Anderson

The total expenses for the town the first year were $55.04.

The following statistics on Eden Prairie were also found in Dr. Neill's "History of Hennepin County":

Total number of acres in the township	19,783	
Assessed valuation of the land	1869	$ 87,373
	1875	$174,766
	1881	$266,303
Personal property value	1869	$ 26,737
	1875	$ 30,116
	1880	$ 38,293
Total taxes	1869	$ 2,314
	1875	$ 2,486
	1880	$ 2,412
Horses over two years old	1869	156
	1875	230
	1880	284
Cattle over two years old	1869	448
	1875	564
	1880	498
Sheep	1869	500
	1875	112
	1880	391
Hogs	1869	125
	1875	112
	1880	313
Wheat	1869	22,593 bushels
	1875	28,107 bushels
	1880	acreage 3,529
Population by the town census of 1880	749	

After the Miller Brothers store was built in the 1870s near the tracks on County Road 4 the town board held its meetings in the hall above the store. This became the polling place for the local, county, state and federal elections. The annual town board meeting was held the first Tuesday after the first Monday in March. This was a convenient time as it came just before the farmers started their field work and the spring break-up of the roads hadn't begun.

The farmers came in sleighs and cutters, tied their horses to the hitching posts around the store and climbed the flight of stairs on the north side of the store to the hall above. The hall was warm and cozy from the heat of the potbellied stove in the corner of the room. There was always a warm lunch served either by the ladies of the Methodist Church or by Kate Miller.

The annual town meetings usually were held in the early afternoon. Here one found the kind of grass-roots democracy in which anyone could get up and express complaints or opinions on any issue pertaining to the town. Motions were made and acted upon. The budget for the year was read, discussed and voted on. Some folks remember the concern when the town budget reached eight thousand dollars. (What would they think of the Eden Prairie city budget for 1979: $2,196,000?) A number of appointments were made. There always seemed to be a joke connected with the appointment of the "pound master," referred to by some as the "dog catcher." Usually, a representative from Hennepin County was present to explain new road constructions and other matters common to both governing bodies. With the adjournment of the meeting the people filed out of the hall. Many would not see each other again until the next annual town board meeting.

The duties of the first town boards may seem simple but they were vital to the time. The appointive position of the two "fence viewers" is an example. The responsibility of these two men was to view all line fences to see that they were constructed so as to prevent livestock from getting out. Reports were made to the town board by these fence viewers. They were also responsible for stray animals in the town.

The Eden Prairie Historical Society has on file a book entitled "Estray Book for the Town of Eden Prairie, Hennepin County,

State of Minnesota, Commencing with November, A.D. 1871," by George Cornwell, town clerk. It contains notices to the town on stray livestock and the reports of a line viewer and another town official. Here is one such notice:

Nov. 1, 1871

To whom it may concern:

Take notice that on Wednesday, the first day of November, A.D., 1871, upon my premises or those I have charge of in Eden Prairie, County of Hennepin, and State of Minnesota, I took up an Estray, and now have in my possession the following described animals: one large red and white cow, apparently about nine years old, one brass nob on the left horn. One last spring or summer heifer calf, red with a white spot on the forehead and a white spot on each flank.

The owner or owners are requested to prove property, pay charges, and take them away.

O.J. Brown

Eden Prairie
Nov. 1, 1871

* * *

We two of the fence viewers of the Town of Eden Prairie do hereby certify that in pursuance of a notice given by O.J. Brown, we proceeded to the O.J. Brown farm and after an examination of the matter specified in said notice we appraised the value of said Estrays as follows:

Description of Estray: a red and white cow with a knob on the left horn, age about 9 years. One red calf with a spot on the forehead and a white spot on each flank.

Damage up to Nov. 1, $2.00
For keeping three weeks $3.75
For posting notices and notifying fence viewers and recording $1.50
Cow appraised at $24.00
Calf appraised at $4.00

Smith mileage $.60   appraisal $.25
Goodrich mileage
$.80   appraisal $.25

Dated at Eden Prairie this 23rd day of Nov. 1871

Sheldon Smith   Supervisors
Horace Goodrich

* * *

In that day they also had dog problems. Packs of dogs would attack flocks of sheep or get into a chicken yard and do considerable damage. The constable was authorized to shoot any troublesome dogs found not to be registered by the town. The Eden Prairie Historical Society has a book entitled, "Register of Dog Licenses for the Town of Eden Prairie, 1882."

The book shows the names of dog owners, the day, month and year a license was issued and date the license expired, the name of the dog with its age, sex, color, weight, breed and the cost of the registration, which was one dollar. In 1882, there were fifty-seven dogs registered in Eden Prairie.

One of the first town clerk books kept by James Gamble, one of the first settlers in Eden Prairie, records the names of those who paid a $1.50 poll tax and the names of those who chose to work on the roads instead. From what we have been able to find out, able-bodied men either had to pay a poll tax or work it out on the roads. At that time the Indian trails were being upgraded. The equipment of the time was crude. A man would tie two split logs together, place a couple of boulders on top to hold them down, and then hitch the logs to a team of horses. This road maintenance was not very successful as there was no one to supervise the work. The action of the town board was to appoint a road supervisor and set up a "road and bridge fund." The town bought four graders at this time and placed one in each corner of the town. Neighbors got together and graded the roads in their particular area.

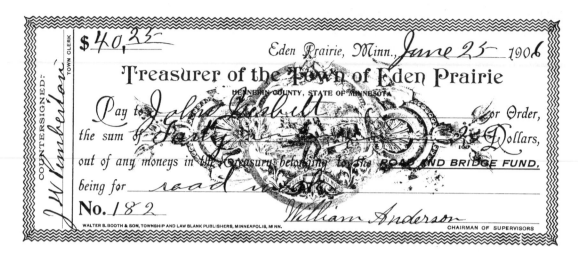

Township Road and Bridge Fund.

As time went on, new and better roads were demanded by the people. The town board contracted with local men to build them. The wheelers, dump wagons, scrapers and other equipment were all pulled by horses. Wages were about thirty-five cents per hour for a man and thirty-five cents per hour for a team. Getting these jobs was competitive as many farmers wanted them to supplement their farm income. Later, outside contractors were hired. Construction camps were set up in the area of construction work: large tents for the horses and bunkhouses for the men. Larger and better road equipment was now used but they continued to keep horses on the jobs until the 1930s.

The Overseer of the Poor

The town paid out very little money for the care of the poor. In the first place, it was considered a disgrace to approach the town board for help. If a family was in need the neighbors helped them out. Then, the town board of that day knew almost all the people in town personally so it wasn't hard to size up a situation. If there was an able-bodied man in the household they'd get him a job on the road or on a farm. Arthur Miller remembered that sometimes the Indians on the river bottoms ran out of food and would come to the Miller Brothers store. His dad would give them what they needed and send the bill to the town.

Aged parents held places of respect in every household and were expected to be cared for by their children. Those who had no home were sent to the Hennepin County Poor Farm on County Road 18 near Hopkins. Those who were able worked in the large barn, vegetable gardens and helped maintain the building and grounds. It gave them a feeling of contributing to their board and lodging. There were paupers lots in both the Pleasant Hill and Eden Prairie cemeteries. The town cared for its own to the end.

For more than fifty years the town board met in Millers Hall. When the new consolidated school was built they had their meetings there until the American Legion hall was built on County Road 4 by the railroad tracks. The Legion hall became the polling place for all the elections except school elections, which were held in the school. From the beginning of the organization of the town there had never been an office for the town clerk. All records were kept in the home of the clerk. Many today still remember the rolltop desk in the Elmer Clark home. The same desk was used by his father-in-law, Ed Gamble, and by Ed Gamble's father, James Gamble, before him.

The Feel of Change

When the automobile replaced the horse and buggy better roads were demanded.

Hennepin County found it needed to keep up with the growing demand for new roads in Eden Prairie and throughout the entire county. Eden Prairie was completely split open when State Highway 169 was built through the middle of the town.

Now Eden Prairie began to move on wheels. Twin City milk trucks criss-crossed the prairie picking up Grade A milk. Vegetable and berry farmers loaded their trucks and headed for the Farmers Market in Minneapolis at four o'clock in the morning. Truckloads of cattle headed for the South St. Paul stockyards. Orange school buses carried the children to the new consolidated school. Greyhound buses passed through town. People traveled to neighboring towns for groceries and other supplies and the four little general stores closed their doors.

Down came the elevator, the creamery, the blacksmith shop, and the stockyards in the area around Millers store. The mail came out of the Hopkins post office so the trains ceased to stop at the Eden Prairie station. The railroad depot closed. The Miller Brothers bought the depot and water tank and used the lumber for farm buildings. The Miller store was the last to close its door. People just had to stop in to visit Kate Miller, that gracious little white-haired lady who had spent all her married life with her family in that store. Few knew, understood and loved the folks in Eden Prairie better than Kate Miller. Kate died in 1950. The store and house remained empty for more than ten years, a ghost of the past. On December 5, 1963, the store, house and grandmother Miller's house went up in flames. It was a historic site that should have been preserved.

Eden Prairie Becomes a Village

Farms in neighboring communities were being sold for industrial and housing developments. But Eden Prairie, with its good agricultural land and progressive farming practices, was slow in giving in to the developers and becoming part of the urban scene.

The first big sign of change came to Eden Prairie with the construction of Flying Cloud Airport in 1946. Soon many found that Eden Prairie was a desirable location for industry with its facilities for motor vehicle, rail and air transportation. Land speculators were again in Eden Prairie and housing developments began to spring up in different parts of the town, bringing new people into the community.

All this put new demands on the local town board and they found it hard to keep abreast of the changes taking place. They saw land-use problems ahead and felt something must be done. One step forward was the appointment of a zoning commission with Arthur Miller as its first chairman. Next, a building inspector was appointed and a strict building code authorized.

New residents wanted to become involved in the local governmental process so an Eden Prairie Citizens League was organized. Their first study was on the potential change in the form of government from that of a township to a village—for whenever a township passed the two thousand population mark, as Eden Prairie did in the 1960 census, a review of the local government is made by the Minnesota Municipal Commission (MMC).

The town board, the Citizens League, and the MMC worked together on this problem. Three options were recommended by the MMC:

1. Remain a township.

2. Incorporate the entire township as a village.

3. Divide the township and incorporate in parts or annex to adjoining municipalities.

The commission indicated that the Eden Prairie town board had done more than others reviewed by the MMC to prevent serious land-use troubles, but pointed out that the town could expect troubles in the future if it did not continue to keep abreast of changes and developments.

**Miller Brothers General Store. West of County Road
4 and south of the railroad tracks.**

The prospect of a change in the local form of government stimulated much community interest and a number of meetings were called by the Citizens League. The League always pointed out that it would not take a stand on the question. It was their duty to present the facts. Advantages of the change to the village status were described as the following:

1. Protecting the community borders from annexation by adjoining municipalities.

2. Permitting the appointment of the assessor, clerk and treasurer who were now elected.

3. Obtaining state funds for roads not available to a township.

The Citizens League ultimately recommended that the village form of government might be the best way to stay ahead of the local problems.

As a result of these public hearings a special election was called in October, 1962, at which time the people of Eden Prairie voted to incorporate the township into the Village of Eden Prairie. On January 1, 1963, the Village of Eden Prairie took over the government of the 36-square-mile area.

The first officials elected for the Village of Eden Prairie in 1962 were: mayor, Donald A. Rogers; clerk, Elmer Clark; councilmen, Kenneth E. Anderson, Alvin J. Bren and Albert J. Bruce; treasurer, Rolf E. Haugen; justice of the peace, William Marshall; and constables, Leslie Kopesky and Norman Larson.

Eden Prairie's first village hall was built in 1964 and is located on Eden Prairie Road (County Road 4). For the first time since the organization of the town, there was a place to keep the town's records.

**Interior of Miller Brothers Store. In the picture are
Norman Miller and Aldene Miller Hobbs.**

The Tuckey home south of Pioneer Trail on Purgatory Creek. Entrance to the store and post office on the right. Note the Tuckey's first log cabin home in the background.

Eden Prairie Post Offices

During the navigation season of 1853, steamboat arrivals occurred almost weekly. The steamboats brought settlers to Bloomington, Eden Prairie, Shakopee and on up the river. At the same time, a new means of travel and communication with the outside world came when a stage line was put in operation between St. Paul and Mankato. The stage stopped at Bloomington Ferry before it crossed the river and followed the Indian trail to Shakopee.

In January, 1854, Joseph Dean established the first post office in Hennepin County at Bloomington Ferry, just two days before John H. Stevens opened a post office in Minneapolis. In the same year Jonas Staring opened a post office in the front part of his home on Staring Lake and served as postmaster. When Horace Goodrich built his store and hall nearby, the post office was relocated in the store. Mr. Staring served as postmaster for fourteen years when Mr. Goodrich's son, Fred, took over the postmaster job.

Mr. Staring's son, Myron, was the first mailman in Eden Prairie. He walked the six miles to meet the stage at Bloomington Ferry and received twelve dollars a year for his services. There is a story about young Myron acquiring a stove pipe hat in which he carried the mail so that his hands were free as he walked the lonely trail. When she saw the black hat above the waving grain, the pioneer housewife knew the mail was on its way.

To meet the needs of the rest of the township, three other post offices were established. To serve the northeastern area a post office was located in the Rowland store and was called the Rowland Post Office. This store building is still standing and is the home of Mr. and Mrs. C. L. Sutton, 7170 Flying Cloud Drive. The second post office was called the Washburn Post Office and was located in the Rankins store, which was southwest of the railroad tracks on County Road 4. When Fred Miller bought the Rankins store and the surrounding land, he built a new store and hall south of the tracks. The post office was relocated in this store and the name was changed to the Eden Prairie Post Office. To accommodate the people in the southeastern part of the township, Henry Tuckey opened a store in the front part of his large home located on Purgatory Creek just across the road from the old Eden Mills. He acquired the right to operate a post office which became known as the Tuckey Post Office.

When the Minneapolis-St. Louis railroad was built through Eden Prairie in 1871 all the mail was dropped off at the Eden Prairie depot located just a short walk east of County Road 4. The law required that bids must be taken for the job of carrying the mail. A bidder had to take a loyalty oath, an oath of securities, obtain a certificate from the postmaster of each post office he served, and in Eden Prairie provide a $300 bond.

Fred Miller served as postmaster for forty-seven years when his son, Fred, Jr., took over the job. Records show that Ezra Paine and Emil Pauly carried the mail for a time, but the best remembered mailman was Harry Neill, who served as Eden Prairie's mailman for thirty-six years.

There was no rural free delivery when Harry Neill first hitched up his horse and buggy and set out with several pouches of mail. Instead, he carried the mail three times a week from one post office to another in a wide swing about the township. Patrons called for their mail at the nearest post office.

With the coming of rural free delivery in 1902, the four post offices consolidated into one post office located in the Miller Brothers store. Two routes were created; Harry Neill was assigned to one covering the south half of Eden Prairie and Ezra Paine to one covering the north half.

Horace F. Goodrich's General Store located on Pioneer Trail where the ball parks on Flying Cloud field are to day. Sketch by Dale Redpath.

Rowland Store and Post Office owned and operated by Frank E. Miller (no relation to Fred F. Miller). This is now the home of Mr. and Mrs. C. L. Sutton, 7170 Flying Cloud Drive.

In the early days Neill experienced his share of hardships common to all pioneer carriers of Uncle Sam's mail. Stories are told of the times he was literally snowbound by arctic blizzards; how he traveled across country and over rail fences, his horses sinking deep in the white drifts; and how he sloshed through sticky mud on the wagon trails to deliver the daily mail. In the horse-and-buggy days he sometimes took along a foot warmer. At times, when he reached home he was close to exhaustion from the cold and exposure. His first car was a sporty 1917 model. He wore out nine cars before his retirement.

Harry Neill was a very accommodating man who had established a friendly relationship with all the folks along his twenty-nine-mile route. It has been said that he not only carried mail but groceries and town gossip as well. Folks would call up Miller's store and request they send along a sack of sugar or some bread with Harry, who would drop it off at the mailbox with the mail. He did this for many years until Uncle Sam found out and said, "No, Harry, you can't do this anymore. It's against the law."

In 1934, the Post Office Department decided to combine the Eden Prairie and Hopkins offices. Naturally, this met with disapproval from the folks in Eden Prairie. A petition was circulated by the town board

Interior of Rowland Store

and sent to the postmaster general in Washington, but it didn't help. The Hopkins post office was notified that it would assume the distribution of the mail over the Eden Prairie routes beginning October 1, 1934. Harry Neill was out of a job.

The people of Eden Prairie felt they should honor Neill for the years of service he had given the community. A big celebration was held at the Eden Prairie Methodist Church. Friends and neighbors gathered to pay tribute and say thank-you to the man who had brought them their mail for more than a third of a century.

People moving into Eden Prairie did not like having a Hopkins address. When the township became a village, the residents started demanding that their address be Eden Prairie. Working with their U.S. congressmen, this was accomplished in 1965. The first post office was set up in the village hall, but it proved to be unsatisfactory so a new location was found in the "Li'l Red" grocery store at the corner of Valley View Road and County Road 4.

Eden Mills

One for the blackbird,
 one for the crow,
One for the cutworm,
 and one to grow

Thus sang the farmer as he dropped the seeds into the fertile ground. The prairie farmer's intimacy with the soil had taught him that not every seed that goes into the earth grows; not every seed bears fruit. In spite of these setbacks, the farmers in Eden Prairie were able to produce more grain than any other town in Hennepin County during the late 1800s and early 1900s. Hennepin Landing was the chief shipping point for the wheat that was sent down the river to the mills at St. Anthony on the small steamboats that plied the Minnesota River. Peter Ritchie, who owned land near the town of Hennepin, was engaged in the shipping business, using his barges to haul wheat and hay to St. Anthony Falls.

Not all the grain went down the river, for to meet the needs of the local farmers a grist mill on Mill Creek (Purgatory Creek) north of Pioneer Trail was built in 1865 by Dr. Nathan Stanton, who had come to this area for his health. He had problems financing his mill so he sold it to Isaac Crowe, an attorney and land speculator in St. Anthony. Crowe owned most of the land which today is the Olympic Hills Golf Course. Dr. Stanton and a Daniel Robertson operated the mill for Crowe until Crowe's death in 1872 when James Till bought it from the heirs. It was sold to J. Balme in 1878. Historical references give the name, Eden Mills, but local residents remember it as the Happy Hollow Mill.

The mill had two runs of stone. One run could produce one hundred barrels of flour in twenty-four hours. The mill used water power only until about 1890 when low water compelled the partial use of steam.

A Mr. Dudley constructed a building near the mill for the double purpose of store and hotel. This property passed into the hands of A. J. Apgar, who kept the hotel open but closed the store. It was destroyed by fire in 1872. Henry Tuckey built a large house across the road from the mill in 1874. The front part housed a store and post office. The mill, store and post office provided a little community center for southeastern Eden Prairie.

The Isaac Crowe files in the manuscript department of the Minnesota Historical Society contain tax receipts and records of amounts and prices of grain sold at the mill. Some flour was shipped to Fort Gibson, Mississippi, where Mr. Crowe owned a cotton plantation. Here are a few of the letters pertaining to the operation of the mill:

* * *

Eden Mills April 27, 1866

I. Crowe, Esqr.

Dear Sir,
We want a crow bar and heavy sledge, some shovels too. Clark had ought to let me know that he was going to town, then I could send for things. I have been looking for you to come out or I would have wrote sooner. I have been digging some stones. It is a job on account that they are so large and heavy to handle. I think we ought to have an ox team, a heavy pair, for the stones is so heavy to handle. I think we ought to have a stone boat as the stones is so heavy that they can't be loaded on a wagon.

Registered letter for Edward Gamble, Rowland Post Office.

Feed is high, too. It will cost any way we try to manage it. Don't you think it will be best to let James Clark built the mill by the job, that is the carpenter work, and for him to furnish the timber, what it will want. Then, we can build the wall and dam. Then we will have the mill and dam ready by the first of July.

You come out when you think you can or write me. Send a sledge and crow bar as soon as you can. We want a heavy sledge. One we can handle easy. No money,

Daniel Robertson

*   *   *

Eden Mills, Oct. 20, 1866

I. Crowe, Esqr.

Dear Sir;

J.J. and myself had to borrow last Thursday $62—to me a note in the bank payable next Thursday and our dependence to pay is on you. We did not call you for those barrels as you were spending so much and would not call now if we could help it. I am very destitute and need what little pittance I can gather up to silence the wants again.

Please pay J.J.
N. Stanton

*   *   *

Eden Prairie Mills, Feb. 26, 1867

I. Crowe, Esqr.

Sir;

The next day after I wrote you I went down to start the mill as I always go down and try it by hand before I put on the water. It did not start easy so I took my light and went into the wheel house and found the west end of the wheel shaft loose. I went over to the ditch and got Mr. Robertson and we worked from Thursday to Saturday night and got it fixed. It runs well now.

I would like a piece of land with plenty of meadow and timber and not have to go quite out of civilization. I suppose you have just the kind of piece of land I want—about 160 acres. I would like to buy it and pay for it in work. You have tried me long enough by this time to know whether I will suit you as your miller. I want a house of my own and have saved every cent to bring me to this point. I will work as hard as my strength will let me. I bought these colts thinking I could raise my own team and have them ready by the time I could get the farm paid for. I have quit the use of tobacco, coffee, tea, and sugar for this purpose. Please answer if this arrangement suits you. A Mr. Livingston wants to sell you some barrells for wheat. He wants 70¢ a barrell. They are all oak except the heads.

I am respectfully yours,
J. Stanton

It seemed that at times there was not enough water in the creek to run the mill, so plans were made to dig a ditch from Neill Lake to Mill Creek. This met with some opposition from the neighboring farmers.

Eden Prairie Mills, Jan. 11, 1867

I. Crowe, Esqr.

Sir:

Mr. Woods, Robert Anderson and William Anderson was over this week to see about digging the ditch and forbid us digging the ditch. They said you must not drain the water until you paid for their damages, and they agreed to go and see you about these damages. They also said they would put a bulk head and go it above yours and stop the water. I saw Robert Anderson to-day. He said he was going to see you next Monday and I think you better not give them in writing that you won't drain but 2 inches of water a year from those lakes. I think you will want more. You better put them off as

61

*easy as you can and have them wait
tell they receive damages. I heard today that two of the Andersons want
the lake drained off so they can have
meadow. They also told me that they
were going to serve a writing note as to
stop us digging the ditch until they
had their pay for damages and they
told others, also. We commenced digging yesterday. It is very hard—froze
2½ ft. deep. Robert Anderson told me
he had seen a lawyer on the case and
said you can't take water from the
farmers, and, also, that congress
could not pass such a law. I am going
to put that ditch through in spite of
them. They can't do any harm by talking. Don't tell them that I wrote you
about this matter.*

*Yours in haste,
Daniel Robertson*

Charles Ree's Pottery

In our modern world where foodstuffs and other commodities are packaged for convenience we tend to forget the pioneer era in which most materials were shipped in bulk containers, such as barrels, to the general stores. The people produced, processed and stored their staples in stoneware ceramic pots, jars and jugs. Butter was churned in a stoneware churn, stored in crocks in a spring house or cool cellar. Sauerkraut and pork were pickled in brine and kept in large stoneware pots. Eggs were preserved in jars of water glass. Molasses, syrup, and other sweeteners were often kept in jugs. Bread was mixed in a ceramic bowl. Mothers' cookies were stored in a stoneware cookie jar.

This was an age in which stoneware was far more important than we can realize today. The need for these containers continued to increase as more households were formed and the population grew. Even when the railroads came, stoneware was somewhat difficult to ship to remote areas as it was bulky, heavy and breakable. Therefore, potteries sprang up in many localities and flourished until driven out of business by more efficient competitors.

The needs of Eden Prairie were met when Charles Rees began making pottery on his farm, Elmwood, in about 1858. This pottery factory was located on Purgatory Creek where Northrup King now has its headquarters. This factory was operated on a modest scale and probably supplemented the Rees farm income. Written records show that Charles Rees supplied flower pots, milk crocks, butter jars and jugs for the surrounding area.

An 1873 map of Eden Prairie shows that the George Brum farm was the former Rees farm. A call to Wesley Brum in Edina revealed that his grandfather bought the farm from Charles Rees. Wesley remembered the old kiln and piles of old pottery and brick on Purgatory Creek and the excavations that ran seventy-five to one hundred feet into the bank along the creek. As time went on, these excavations were filled as cows and pigs would get in them and it was a problem getting them out. He remembered his grandfather telling him that the quality of the clay was poor and could not compete with the clay found in the Red Wing, Minnesota, area.

The Railroads

Eden Prairie was part of the river frontier and was settled in the steamboat era. The first years were lonely for those people, especially between the time the river closed and the ice went out in the spring. The answer to year-around communication with the outside world was railroads.

This era began on June 28, 1862 when the state's first ten-mile track was opened between St. Paul and St. Anthony. The first locomotive was the William Crooks, named after the chief engineer of the Minnesota and Pacific Railroad—the company that built the road. This locomotive traveled by rail to LaCrosse, Wisconsin and then was transported from there to St. Paul by Mississippi River boat. The ten miles of track covered by the William Crooks on that June day were symbolic, for from then on railroads began to spread throughout the state and carried immigrants into the rich farmlands.

When the Minneapolis-St. Louis railroad was built through Eden Prairie in 1871 and the Hastings-Dakota (Milwaukee) in 1881, commerce left the river. Business establishments naturally sprang up along the railroad track. A depot was built near the middle of the town in section 17, just east of County Road 4 on the Minneapolis-St. Louis line.

Two local men recalled their childhood days spent in the area around the depot and the railroad tracks:

Arthur Miller's Story

"The first railroad tracks were built with local labor using wheelbarrows, wagons, oxen, and the few horses that could be rounded up. It was a very winding track with steep grades out of Chaska. When an engine was hauling a long string of cars, the engineer often would take some of the cars up the grade and put them on the side track at Eden Prairie and return for the rest of the cars. There was a big trestle over Highway 101 near Shakopee and another one over

Eden Prairie Depot and Water Tank. Painting by Adolph (Dutch) Popowske.

Purgatory Creek at the Stacy place. These trestles were built of heavy timber. When the railroad was straightened by the Walsh Construction Company in 1901-1902, these trestles were filled with dirt. There were camps of railroad workers along the track— two hundred or more men. My Father, proprietor of the Miller Brothers General Store, furnished supplies for these camps. The men worked with dump cars and steam shovels.

"The first trains had steam boilers and were fired by wood. Father sold wood to the railroad. Piles of cordwood lined the tracks. There was a water tank and pumping station north of the tracks. A Mr. Pollack was the pumper. He'd pump water for the trains at Eden Prairie and then ride up to Marion Junction and pump for the trains up there. He would then catch a train back to Eden Prairie and start pumping all over again. That was one tough job. There was a ditch from Red Rock Lake to the tank by the tracks. For a time a windmill was used to pump the water; but after the railroad was straightened, a new water tank was built and a six-inch well was drilled. Now the water was pumped by steam motor. This six-inch well is still by the track."

63

The David Frank Douglas House on County Road 4. Now owned by Mr. and Mrs. Earl R. More.

Sheldon Douglas' Story

"My grandfather, Sheldon Smith, preempted land north of Duck Lake in 1855. He served as township treasurer for a number of years. His daughter, Annie, married my father, David Frank Douglas, a school teacher, in 1890. My parents built that beautiful red brick house with the white trim located north of the Legion Hall on County Road 4. My father built five rooms upstairs in this house. This was to accommodate travelers who got off at the Eden Prairie station. At this time the only way for people to get to the Chanhassen-Excelsior area was to get off at Eden Prairie. They often stayed at our Douglas House and then Father would take them by stage to their destination.

"The first depot agent in Eden Prairie was R. O. Reed, followed by my grandfather, Sheldon Smith; my mother, Annie Smith Douglas; Beckey Hunter Hamilton; a Miss Newell; and Agnes Jarrett. My father and Mother studied telegraphy and Mother trained all the telegraphers who served as depot agents. This area around the depot became the center of community activity. There was the Miller's General Store, the creamery, the blacksmith shop, the grain elevator and the cattle pens by the tracks.

"I served a number of years on the school board during those trying days of consolidation. One of the reasons for the choice of location for the first consolidated school, No. 141 (now the middle school) was the accessibility to the railroad. Each year about three carloads of coal were placed on the side track. Local men bid on the job of hauling the coal and filling the coal bins at the school. This first was done by wagon and in winter by sled.

"I remember the fascination the trains had for the young boys in the area and the fun we had swimming in the water tank. But we had to be on the alert for a train might come along and take the water before we had a chance to get out."

The Rural Schools

Pioneer schoolmaster James Gamble used the sitting room of his log cabin for a school and taught the "three R's" to the boys and girls of the neighborhood. By 1857, more room was needed, so James Anderson donated an acre of land for the first school in Eden Prairie. The site was where Sears south parking lot is today.

The men of the neighborhood gathered and erected a little log structure, eighteen by twenty-five feet in size. It had three windows—one at the teacher's desk and one on each side of the room. The teacher's desk was a large box with a shelf in it. A large stove sat in the center of the room. Plank seats were built against the walls. Serving as desks were planks built up in front of the plank seats.

Martha Paine, daughter of William Paine, was the first teacher. Among her first pupils were John, Mary and Lizzie Gamble; John Anderson; and Ezra and John Paine.

John W. Anderson, son of James Anderson. One of the first six students to attend the Anderson Log school. His entire life of 95½ years was lived in Eden Prairie.

After the township of Eden Prairie was organized in 1858 the town board appointed James Gamble superintendent of the common schools. In 1860 he defined the boundary lines for the four original school districts: Gould School, District 56; Anderson School, District 55; Wolf School, District 57; and Jarrett School, District 54. Each school district had a three-member school board and was named after the people who either donated the land or sold the land to the town for sums ranging from ten to twenty-five dollars.

Mr. Gamble served as superintendent until the county commissioners appointed the first superintendent of schools on September 7, 1864.

In the 1860s classes were held only three months out of the year as the children were needed at home for farm work. Books were scarce and textbooks were hard to come by. Families valued them and parents gave their children the books when they were old enough to go to school. By the 1870s the state paid a St. Paul publisher to supply a series of inexpensive textbooks for schools. These books wouldn't excite many students today. There were few pictures, the words were difficult and the writers didn't try very hard to make the subjects interesting. But the students liked them as they were the only books they knew. Each book was a treasure. Each word was a challenge. Learning to read and write was an important victory and anyone who had learned to add or subtract was thought of as being even more remarkable.

At first there were no specific educational qualifications for teachers other than a desire to teach and later pass an examination for a teachers certificate. The county commissioners gave the examinations. Many persons with less than an eighth-grade education could teach if they passed the examination. One of the first duties of the newly elected county superintendent of schools was to give the teachers examination. Ten points on the examination was rated per-

Jarrett School.

Loring Tuckey, son of Henry Tuckey, was a teacher in the Jarrett School in the early 1900's.

Gould School.

fect. Zero was failure. Subjects included on the examination were orthography (art of writing words with proper letters according to standard usage and correct spelling), reading, arithmetic (mental), writing, theory, grammar, physical geography, geography, algebra, arithmetic, history and geometry.

Later, a high-school education was required before taking the examination. Then a one-year normal course after high school was required to teach in a rural school.

The teachers were expected to live exemplary lives. Women teachers were expected to be home at a certain hour and were expected to quit teaching when they married. Men teachers were forbidden to enter local taverns or to engage in card games, plus avoid the use of tobacco. All teachers were expected to be in church on Sunday morning and attend all respectable social functions in the community.

Anderson School.

"BACK TO THE FARM"
A PLAY IN THREE ACTS
Given by Young People of Jarrett and Gould Schools
MILLER'S HALL, EDEN PRAIRIE
SATURDAY, MAY 6, 1922
8:30 p. m.   Adults 50c

School Play.

Wolf School.

Homer Raquet, a lifetime resident of Eden Prairie, heard his mother tell about the first schools as she had been a teacher at the Gould School. In 1927, when Homer was a sophomore at Hopkins High School, he wrote an essay on local history which was published in the Hennepin County Review, the local newspaper. It read as follows:

The Gould School was built in 1858 and was named after Aaron Gould who donated the land. It was a one room building built of tamarack logs. The desks were mere log benches built along the walls all the way around the room. In this way there was room for more pupils. The stove was in the center of the room and on cold days the pupils sat around it to keep warm. The pupils were all the way from six to twenty-one years old. Some of the children would get gum from the tamarack logs. Thus, even the first teachers had trouble with chewing gum.

The first teacher was Thomas James and he taught a three month term which was held in the winter. These early settlers were poor and needed the older boys and girls at home to help about the farm and make clothing

for the rest of the family. The teacher had to wait until school closed for his pay which was only $15 a month. The teachers boarded around with the children's parents, spending a week or more according to the number of children sent to school. Those sending no children did not have to board

Jesse Cleland (Mrs. David Clark) taught in the Wolf School around the year 1905.

the teacher. The parents sending children to school also had to furnish wood and water. All these things helped keep some children away from school. The number of pupils sent to this school was anywhere from thirty to fifty-five. Some had to walk as far as four miles one way. The school was also used for the Methodist Church until a church building was built in 1872.

The schoolhouse door was left open on warm days so as to have some direct ventilation. It was a common thing for a cow to walk along the road and give a gentle moo at the open door and look about at the laughing faces. One day the boys put a barrel on a cow's head and kept her near the schoolhouse until the teacher rang her little bell. The boys went inside and were soon busy studying. They heard the cow hitting his head against the schoolhouse, trying to get the barrel off. Finally the cow managed to get the barrel off. The boys were always planning some funny jokes or tricks which the children would all laugh at.

All the four schools in Eden Prairie were log buildings until new schools were built between 1870-1875. These new buildings had many new things such as double and single desks, a stove with a jacket around it, and a method of ventilation through the chimney. The teachers now taught seven months a year and boarded full time at one house. She was paid once a month.

The subject of consolidation arose about 1900 but was not completed until 1916. Because of the war years they did not vote on bonds for several years. In 1920 they began a regular campaign for an $80,000 bond. Some thought it was too high. Others wanted only eight grades while some joked and said, "Why don't you build a university for your bright boys and girls."

The school was completed in 1924. It was used for the eight grades and two years of high school. The cost came to almost three times the bonds but Eden Prairie had one of the finest schools in the county. It had the latest ventilating, heating and lighting systems. Buses hauled the children to school and one bus was sent to Hopkins with the juniors and seniors.

Eden Prairie's rapid progress in education shows the way people are willing to pay heavy taxes to give their children a good chance in life and this is gained through a good education.

Marion Rogers, the Country School Teacher

The year was 1919 and Marion Russell and a friend, Mary Daly, met with the county superintendent because they had heard of openings in the Gould and Anderson schools in Eden Prairie. They got the jobs. Marion Russell taught at the Gould School for three years. She married a local young man, Roland Rogers, and raised three boys and one girl, all of whom graduated from the Eden Prairie High School.

"Winter was often felt inside the schoolhouse, especially in the back of the room," recalled Mrs. Rogers. "We would have to put our lunch pails around the stove to thaw them out. There were no electric lights and daylight became pretty dim at times in winter.

"The one-room school with double and single desks held all eight grades. Each class would come to the teacher's desk and recite the day's lesson. Because we had so many subjects to teach, each class would only last ten or fifteen minutes. We just didn't have time to finish a subject the way we wanted to. The younger students learned an awful lot by listening to the older children recite; and then the older students were helpful in teaching the younger students.

"As a general rule the children weren't sassy. Most of the time I would just talk to them—might shake one a little once in a while. The children liked to take trips to the little house out back. I'd have to be careful and watch if it was a necessity trip or a chance to get out of a little work."

She was asked how one teacher managed to control thirty-five or more students of all ages. "Be kind and just, but devilish firm," she answered. "That's what we all used to say."

Marion Rogers recalled that teachers had to do their own janitor work in the one-room school. "On some days the teacher had to wade through snowdrifts to reach the schoolhouse door and start the fire before the students arrived. Often the water pail might be frozen. We had to keep putting wood or coal on the fire all day long. After the children left for home, the teacher had to sweep the floor and straighten the room before she left each day. The school didn't have its own well so water had to be carried from surrounding farms. Some boys got two dollars a month for keeping the water pail full.

"The highlights of the school year were the Christmas programs, spelling bees with neighboring schools and the annual school picnic on the closing day of school."

The Bryant School

One other school in Eden Prairie that should be mentioned is Bryant School, District 60.

William Bryant and his wife, Hannah, first came from New York to St. Anthony and then moved to Eden Prairie in 1854 when they preempted 140 acres of land on what now is called Bryant Lake.

Hannah Bryant started a private school in her log cabin home for her children. She invited the Bohemian children of the neighborhood to also come to her home for lessons. She received no pay, but these neighbors helped Mr. Bryant with the farm work in appreciation for what Hannah did for their children. Soon the home was too small for the number of children who wanted to learn and Mr. Bryant built a little log schoolhouse at the junction of what is now Rowland Road and Shady Oak Road.

Records show that a Sarah Clark taught there in 1856 followed by a Miss Craik of Edina and Alice Bren, sister of Dan Bren.

In order to get state aid for supplies, a school district had to be formed with a qualified teacher in charge. In 1869 that was accomplished and a new building was constructed. On September 7, 1870 Hannah Bryant took her teacher's examination, which qualified her to teach in this new school. Two of her daughters carried on as teachers in this school. First there was Sarah and then Rose.

Some of the children in the northern part of the district had to walk more than three miles to school while others had just a short distance to go. Through the demands of the people in the north, a new school was built across the town line in Minnetonka in 1892. Many wanted to call this the Hannah Bryant School in honor of the first teacher, but the name Shady Oak, District 97, was agreed upon. Later this district merged with the Hopkins School District.

Consolidated School District 141

The subject of consolidating the four rural schools started about 1900. It was the topic of debate at every community gathering. Some favored the idea while others were firmly opposed to it.

The township at that time was divided into four neighborhood communities, each of which centered around their respective one-room school. There was the Wolf School on Pioneer Trail in the southeastern part of the town. The Gould School at the junction of County Road 4 and Pioneer Trail was the center of activity in southwest Eden Prairie. The Jarrett school was located where Immanuel Lutheran Church is today and was the gathering place for people in the northwest area. People in the central and northeastern part of the township were identified with the Anderson School. Each neighborhood was proud of its own school and the people liked the intimacy that existed between teacher, student and parent.

Consolidated School District No. 141. Painting by Doty Nye, teacher in the Eden Prairie Schools for twenty-five years.

Library in the Consolidated School. Mrs. Robert Lucas was the first librarian.

Fifth grade class, 1946–47.

But the trend of the time was to combine small rural schools into larger districts. As a result, more money would be available to build better buildings, hire more qualified teachers and improve libraries and other facilities.

The first formal meeting on consolidation took place at Miller's Hall on May 29, 1916, after which each district petitioned the county superintendent to consider the consolidation of the four rural schools. On September 11, 1916, a special election was held at Miller's Hall. There were 150 qualified voters: 124 for consolidation and 26 against.

World War I became a big issue in the town and people were preoccupied with Liberty Loan and War Savings Bond drives, so it wasn't until 1920 that a bond drive was made for the new school. The bond issue passed but the school board had failed to include a vote on the site of the new school —an oversight that caused fireworks. The school board and the people could not agree on a site and the community became divid-

ed over the issue. Sheldon Douglas was chairman of the board at that time. He and the rest of the board favored property belonging to Mr. Douglas near the railroad tracks where the middle school is today. Others favored the Wilson Mitchell site at the junction of Mitchell Road and Scenic Heights Road as it was more centrally located and was on level ground, whereas one had to climb a hill to get to the Douglas site.

Arthur Miller was active in community affairs at that time. Here is his description of the temper of the town:

"This town was really hot. There was civil war in Eden Prairie. There were fistfights. People from the south end of town who favored the Mitchell site wouldn't trade at the Miller Brother's store. Harry Neill, the mailman, all the time was enjoying the situation and kept the pot boiling as he carried gossip from the north to the people in the south part of town.

"There was one board member, James Brown, who lived on the river bluffs in south

School Band, 1934. Armand Christiansen, instructor.

Eden Prairie. He favored the Douglas site and the people in his area gave him a rough time. Some pranksters found some green paint. One night they got into Mr. Brown's barn and painted his horse green. Mr. Brown had to drive around the community with a green horse until the paint wore off. Some people started digging on the Mitchell site to prove where they wanted the school. My dad offered a compromise site where my house now stands but no one was interested.

Finally, the school board said they would put it to the vote of the people. The Douglas site won but the people in the south said it wasn't a fair election. A lawsuit resulted. The issue went to court. I helped the school board get a smart attorney friend of mine from Minneapolis and we won."

Construction of the school started in May, 1922. On March 10, 1924, the four rural schools were closed and the desks and other

usable equipment were moved to the new building. The school was dedicated April 25, 1924. There was an afternoon and evening program with lunch served from four to seven o'clock. State and county educators participated in the well-executed program. Eden Prairie was so proud to show the public that it had one of the finest consolidated schools in the county.

First high school graduation class, 1929.

Opening Program

FOR THE

CONSOLIDATED SCHOOL BUILDING

OF

Independent School District No. 141

EDEN PRAIRIE, MINNESOTA

FRIDAY, APRIL 25, 1924

The School Board

S. F. Douglas, Chairman   J. Dana Pemberton, Clerk
R. E. Jarrett, Treasurer   James A. Brown
John Rogers   C. Q. Page

The School Faculty

Julia A. Simmons, Principal
Seventh and Eighth Grades

Florence Kruger,
Fifth and Sixth Grades

Sarah Ingebritsen
Third and Fourth Grades.

Esther Anderson
First and Second Grades.

Dedication Program for the new Consolidated School District No. 141.

The school was for the first eight grades and two years of high school. The juniors and seniors went to Hopkins High School by bus. Each year more classes were added until there was a full four-year high-school program. The members of the school's first graduating class in 1929 were Florence Anderson, Rose Anderson, Stanley Anderson, Mary Frissell, Esther Moran, Helen Pavelka and Isabel Tobias. I.O. Frisvold was the superintendent.

Eden Prairie's first conference basketball team. Left to right: Albert Picha, Oliver Anderson, Arthur Watkins, Chester Neill, Stanley Anderson.

At first there were four grade-school teachers, each teaching two grades, and three high-school teachers plus a part-time music teacher and agricultural teacher from Hopkins High School. Teachers had many extra duties besides classroom teaching. For example, Sherman A. Mitchell, superintendent from 1930 to 1940, taught a history class, coached the boys basketball team and substituted as a bus driver along with his duties as superintendent.

Because there were few books for the first library, the school board contracted to have the Hennepin County Library use the school library. The first librarians were in charge of both the school and county books. Mrs. Robert Lucas was the first librarian, followed by Ruth Jarrett Oothoudt. The 1950 school addition provided for a new library. Doty Nye acted as librarian along with her teaching duties. Soon the number of volumes in the school library increased to the point where there wasn't room for the county books. The cooperation was discontinued. The town was then served by the

School buses, 1934. Drivers left to right: Wm. Kutcher, Everett Moran, Elmer Moran, Ted Rogers.

Bookmobile that stopped at designated stops where people gathered to pick up their books.

The community set high standards for their teachers and cooperated in every way to provide the best education possible for their children. The first Parent and Teachers Association was organized April 1, 1925. Salaries of the teachers were low according to today's standards, but the teachers were dedicated to their work. Time spent after school was never considered in a contract. The teachers lived in the community, usually knew the parents of the students person-

ally, and shared the achievements of the students in a very personal way.

This was true of other employees as illustrated by the following interview with Everett Moran, one of the first bus drivers:

"The first bus drivers were me, my brother Elmer, Ted Rogers, and William Kutcher, who was also the janitor. We had four buses. They were all manual transmission. These first buses were made in Chaska and were built mostly of wood and shaped metal. The windows were just ordinary plain glass. They were rough riding and held only thirty or more kids.

"Just as the buses were primitive, so were the roads. As I recall, the town didn't have a snowplow. They decided if they were going to run buses they would have to plow the roads, which were narrow and mostly dirt and gravel. In the spring the ruts would be axle deep and many a time you would get mired down and have to dig your way out. In the winter we used chains. It was quite a job just keeping these chains repaired. If you couldn't make it through some snow drifts, why, you'd just go around them through a field.

"We got thirty-five dollars a month and were expected to maintain the buses and all minor repairs ourselves. During the Depression it was hard to make ends meet. There was no relief in those days and you had to make it or else. We made out.

"When I first started driving, kids realized it was a privilege to ride and therefore were cooperative. The rule was that if you didn't behave we'd open the door and out you'd go. If a child was sick, I'd never think of leaving him off at the mailbox but would drive right up into the yard and see the kid got safely in the house. Later the kids got more destructive. They'd cut up the seats with jackknives. I don't know why they did it. It really bugged me. I tried to correct them myself instead of going to higher authorities. Generally, it worked."

Hot Lunches

Hot lunches were served from a small room built under the east stairway. This room was congested and the ventilation was poor at times but the children will never forget the good food prepared by Mabel Kutcher. Very little went in the garbage can. Mabel knew what children liked and catered to them. About twice a week Mabel would arrive around 6 a.m. with her husband, Bill, the janitor. By ten in the morning the aroma of fresh raised doughnuts or cinnamon rolls came drifting through the halls. There was no lunch room so the children sat on the bleachers in the gym, but there were no complaints.

Growing Pains

Soon the rooms in this building were getting crowded. Additional classrooms, a new library, a music room and a manual training room were needed. Some people felt it would be more economical to again send the high-school students to Hopkins as times were hard and money was scarce. Others, along with the school board, felt an addition should be built. A bond issue was put up to the people to vote on and it passed. It was sufficient to add an addition on the north side of the school in the 1950s. In 1955 a new kitchen, cafeteria, and more classrooms were built on the west end of the building.

The people were now asking for a new gymnasium. The dressing rooms and locker rooms were too small. Some of the boys had to use the boiler room. Attendance at the basketball games had increased to the point where people were packed in like sardines. The fire marshal called the place a firetrap. Some board members wanted to add a wing on the east end of the building while others firmly insisted that there would be no more patchwork construction and that a new separate high school should be built. This was accomplished in 1959 with additions added in 1961 and 1968.

Churches
Eden Prairie Presbyterian Church, 1855-1970

In the summer of 1843, the Pond brothers —Samuel W. and Gidion H.—built a mission house at Oak Grove (Bloomington). There, the Ponds preached to the Indians in the Indians' own language in the morning and to the whites in the afternoon. When the Robert Anderson family arrived in Eden Prairie in 1853 there were no religious services on the prairie. They heard there was preaching at Oak Grove. As they were churchgoing people, they keenly felt the absence of church services. They had nothing but an ox team and thought it would not be appropriate to go to church in such a fashion, so the first time they went to church the

Eden Prairie Presbyterian Church Harvest Festival, 1893. The church was located in front of the Pleasant Hill Cemetery on Pioneer Trail.

Eden Prairie Presbyterian Church Christian Endeavor Society.

Presbyterian Ladies Aid, about 1910.

Andersons, carrying their baby, walked six miles to church and the six miles back home again. The next Sunday, however, they rode nearly to the church with the ox team, hitched the team to a tree in a nearby woods and walked the rest of the way by foot. Shortly after that time, Gideon Pond started holding religious services at the home of Hiram Abbott in Eden Prairie.

The permanent settlers brought with them a love for established religion. They had brought their Bibles and prayer books to read and record family history. But they missed the spiritual strength and fellowship received in a church service. Many of the

Wedding picture of Rev. and Mrs. Walter Finch, June 28, 1893. Rev. Finch grew up in Eden Prairie, attended Macalester College, organized the Christian Endeavor Society, and served as pastor of the Eden Prairie Presbyterian Church in his retirement years.

first settlers had a Scot-Presbyterian background and wished to establish such a church in Eden Prairie. For the story of this first church we'll refer to the "Autobiography of Mary Jane Hill Anderson":

"I want to leave some of my memories of the efforts of the early settlers of Eden Prairie to spread the gospel. The present generation has no idea of the untiring zeal and self-denial the early settlers practiced to leave the two churches—Methodist and Presbyterian—a heritage to their descendants in the community.

"In 1855, Rev. Hugh McHatten of Galena, Illinois was ordered by his doctor to spend a summer in Minnesota because of poor health. Rev. McHatten promised the Anderson relatives in Galena that he would see their Minnesota kinfolk before he came back. He came just after we had built the log schoolhouse on James Anderson's farm. Rev. McHatten preached in this log schoolhouse for about a month that summer. Before going back he told us how to go about organizing a church. He promised to write us about how to contact the General Assembly of the Presbyterian Church so we could apply for pulpit supplies.

"When Rev. McHatten was ready to go back, he came to Father and said 'Mr. Anderson, I cannot go back to Galena. I haven't any money to pay my way back.' Father didn't know what to do. There was no money as no one had sold anything so far that summer. We talked it over and thought of a new neighbor, Richard Neill, who had just come from Canada and bought the William McCoy place. We thought Mr. Neill might have some real money. Father went over and told Mr. Neill the facts and asked for a loan for which he would be personally responsible. Mr. Neill said, 'Yes, I have some money put away to pay a note coming due, but money may come from Canada to meet the note. The poor minister must get home. Take the money.' Richard Neill gave the first money for Presbyterianism in Eden Prairie.

"The next summer, 1856, Rev. Alexander McHatten, a brother of Hugh, came from Galena and organized a United Presbyterian Church. These are the Names of the charter members:

> Mr. and Mrs. James Gamble and Mary Jane
> Mr. and Mrs. Robert Anderson
> Mr. and Mrs. James Anderson
> Mrs. Robin Anderson (mother of the Andersons)
> Samuel, Archie, William, and Fannie Anderson
> Mr. and Mrs. William McCoy
> Mrs. Nancy Steenson, sons, Hugh and William

"Rev. McHatten stayed three months and preached in the log schoolhouse. We had no preaching then until the next summer but we held Sunday School and prayer meetings. These services were conducted by the first two elected elders, James Gamble and Robert Anderson.

"A Rev. McCartney came and preached during the summer of 1857. He was followed by a Mr. Black. Mr. Black had just been married and was sent with his bride up the Mississippi to look after a church that had been started on Lake Pepin. He was to spend three months at each church. At the close of the first service at Lake Pepin, everyone hurried out and left him and his bride standing there with no place to go. She was heart-broken and said, 'Let us go up to Eden Prairie and see what kind of folks are up there.' Well, when they came Mr. and Mrs. James Gamble went to meet them and the young bride got a warm welcome from everyone.

"Mr. Black and his bride decided to stay but there was no house for them. We had a lean-to for a kitchen on our log cabin. We fixed that up for them by putting a partition across. They used the back part for a bedroom and the front for a living room. Father built a shed for our kitchen. I had to go outside to get to this shed and in stormy weather it was pretty hard to carry food back to the house, but even so we all enjoyed it.

"Mr. and Mrs. Black stayed in Eden Prairie for two years. We all felt these were about the happiest years of our lives, although we had the concern of the Civil War and the unrest before the Indian Outbreak of 1862.

"Rev. A. B. Coleman followed Mr. Black. The little schoolhouse was too small for the growing settlement. Rev. Coleman went out to secure subscriptions for a church building. Everyone seemed ready to help. In 1866, Jacob Wolf donated land, a part of his farm. This was near the center of the community (in front of the Pleasant Hill Cemetery on Pioneer Trail). With a site for a church, the little band of worshippers were well on their way; donating time, labor, and money."

In 1869 the first Presbyterian church in Eden Prairie was built—a little frame building twenty-eight by twenty-six feet in size. It was located in Section 26 on County Road 1 (Pioneer Trail). In 1895 an addition to the west was put on and horse sheds were built. In 1900 the women of the church raised money to build a manse across the road from the church.

We must again refer to the "Autobiography of Mary Jane Hill Anderson" for a descriptive account of the building of this first church:

"The building of that little church was a work of self denial. Father was treasurer and kept the records in a pasteboard covered account book. That little book, after nearly three quarters of a century tells an eloquent story of the faith and love of those founders of a Christian community in the wilderness. It is interesting to look back from these modern days of luxury to the pinching hardships endured in raising money for a new church. The account book shows that many contributions were in produce. The prices at which this produce sold seem unbelievable in comparison with values today. Beef brought only four or five cents a pound and other things were in proportion, but all building materials were high. The front door cost $17.00 and the lock and hinges $6.40. It took 160 pounds of beef to pay for those hinges and locks. The big cast iron stove cost $36.00. The lamps which hung from the ceiling, sparkling with prism glass, were the pride of the community. How those prisms flashed and glittered in the light of the kerosene flame. No electric lights ever seemed so wonderful. The children were awe-struck with the beauty of them. The record shows that when the church was finished it cost $1,057 in cash with $259 yet to raise before we could feel our church free of debt. The women of the church put on a great festival and raised this remaining amount."

A big change took place in the worship service in the year 1884 when the congregation voted to discontinue the singing of the Psalms, and hymnals were introduced. A little organ replaced James Gamble's tuning fork. Some of the members objected to this startling change as they felt a musical instrument should not be in a house of worship.

Though this first little church's membership never exceeded 150, it sent seven young men into the ministry, one into YMCA work and three young women into full-time Christian service.

In 1956, the church celebrated its one hundredth anniversary. The slogan for the centennial celebration was "A Century of Faith Turns Toward Tomorrow." Again the members of this little church realized that the demand for service and sacrifice was as great as ever, for the future of the church was now linked with the inevitable growth and development of the community. They went forward and built a new church on Flying Cloud Drive. The building was dedicated June 16, 1960 and a new manse for their pastor was built on Gordon Drive in 1968.

Present Presbyterian Church on Leona Drive and Flying Cloud Drive.

Eden Prairie Methodist Church
1853-1970

The first services of the Methodist church were conducted in the homes of Jonas Staring and David Mitchell. Rev. Bell of Shakopee was the pastor. Soon the little log schoolhouse, the Gould School, became the meeting place. Rev. Charles Galpin of Excelsior followed Rev. Bell as pastor of this embryonic church group. In these humble services God's presence was manifest and the number of members slowly increased.

Rev. John Harrison Macomber was the first appointed pastor. After a series of evangelistic services the society began to feel strong enough to build a house of worship. Sufficient funds were secured for the work to commence. William Collins donated a tract

Macomber Memorial Methodist Episcopal Church south of Pioneer Trail at the junction of County Road 4. Dedicated, June 1872.

of land for the church near the Gould School at the junction of County Road 4 and Pioneer Trail. Rev. Macomber, who was also a carpenter, drew up the plans for the church, supervised the work, and worked four days a week from the time building was begun until the last nail was driven. Lumber was brought out on the Minneapolis-St. Louis Railway that had been laid the year before. Members gave generously of their time and money. Construction was started in the fall of 1871 and resumed the following spring. The cost of its construction was about $1,600, which was paid by the dedication date—June 16, 1872.

Before and at the time the church was being constructed, Eden Prairie and Richfield were sharing a minister. Richfield services were conducted in the morning and the Eden Prairie services were in the afternoon.

The association with Richfield was dissolved and for a short time they were united with Excelsior. At one time the Methodist church and the Presbyterian church shared the same pastor. For a time the church was associated with the Bloomington Methodist church. A number of the pastors at this time were students from Hamline University in St. Paul. These young men would spend the weekend with a church family and the two congregations furnished them with a horse and buggy.

Some of the improvements made to this little church during the years were: a new organ installed in 1875 at the cost of $182; a new furnace and the exterior stuccoed in 1922; and in 1947 the foundation was repaired and some interior improvements were made.

In 1961, with 110 members and fifty families, the congregation moved to its present site at 15051 Scenic Heights Road. The first stage of the building included the sanctuary, kitchen, parlor, restrooms and nursery. The second unit and educational wing with eight classrooms, was completed in 1964. In 1965, the first Methodist parsonage in Eden Prairie history was built. Rev. Alden W. Keiski and his family became the congregation's first parsonage family to live in the community.

From a small group of Methodist families meeting in the log homes of an unestablished community to a growing congregation worshiping in a modern building of a flourishing city, Eden Prairie Methodists have a great heritage to be proud of and a challenging future ahead.

Raymond B. Walker, student pastor from Hamline University. St. Paul. Served the church from 1910 to 1912.

37th Anniversary and Jubilee Service of the Macomber Methodist Episcopal Church, June 16, 1909.

Present sanctuary of the Eden Prairie Methodist Church located on Scenic Heights Road.

Mrs. Robert Lucas wrote a booklet entitled, "A Walk Beside the River of Tomorrow," for the 37th anniversary and Jubilee service of the Macomber Methodist Episcopal Church of Eden Prairie on June 16, 1909. Mrs. Lucas took a prophetic look at the future of Methodism in Eden Prairie back in 1909. It is amazing how many of her hopes and dreams for the church came true. She was not able to know the joy of watching as builders constructed the two church units and the parsonage on her property just a few feet away from the original Lucas homestead.

Mrs. Lucas' little booklet has been an inspiration to the congregation since the day she wrote it and symbolized what every church needs: people who dream, who have the courage to envision what can be done with God's guidance, and who are not afraid of becoming involved in the pain and frustration, the enthusiasm and joy of Christian service.

A copy of Mrs. Lucas' story may be found in the Eden Prairie Methodist Church or the Eden Prairie Historical Society files.

St. John's Episcopal Church in the Wilderness

In the early 1850s there was a corporate body known as the St. Anthony Falls Mission. This mission field covered an area forty miles in width by 125 miles in length. Missionaries sent out by the mission worked in the rural settlements around St. Anthony and the hamlets and villages between Carver on the Minnesota River north to Sauk Rapids.

With a Bible and a prayer book under his arm, the missionary went from log cabin to log cabin as he ministered to the sick, the dying, the lonely and the distressed. His first work was to select points for permanent service and then proceed with the building of a church or small chapel. Within a short time churches had been consecrated at points from Carver to St. Cloud.

St. John's Episcopal Church in the Wilderness was located across from the Flying Cloud Airport on Pioneer Trail. Minnesota Historical Society.

The life of the missionary was rugged. A Rev. Chamberlain, one of the first missionaries, reported making the 140-mile route to Sauk Rapids and back every month, walking the 70 miles to Sauk Rapids and back while holding 20 or more services each month along the way.

Word was received by the mission that there were a number of Episcopalian families living in Eden Prairie. On January 17, 1860 Rev. John A. Fitch was ordered to visit Eden Prairie. Becoming satisfied that it was an encouraging field for missionary work, he arranged for a service in one of the log homes on January 22. In Rev. Fitch's report the following June he stated, "Our place of assembly at present is a barn." On another occasion he reported, "The services were held in a grove by a beautiful lake" (Staring Lake). He also commented, "The beauty of the township and the excellence of the land had attracted an intelligent population at an early age."

Money had been promised for a church building. However, it was never built because the Civil War and the Indian Outbreak of 1862 brought such suffering that many of the members left the community while others could only think of their own survival.

In 1860 a neat little twenty-two by twenty-four-foot frame church was built in the little English settlement of Chanhassen. Rev. Chamberlain, from the St. Anthony Falls Mission, ministered to this group. Among the active members was the C.W. Rees family. Mr. Rees assisted Rev. Chamberlain as a lay reader while his wife was in charge of Sunday school. Their daughter, Louise, assisted the missionary in music at both the Chanhassen church and the Excelsior church.

It was in August of 1862 that word of the Indian outbreak reached the settlement. After the close of divine service one Sunday the members built a stockade around the little church. Here the frightened people stayed while their homes were burned and their cattle driven astray. By the time the fighting ceased, almost the complete settlement had moved away. Rev. Chamberlain left and the church was closed.

In 1866 Mr. Rees, who had since moved to Eden Prairie, thought the people of the community would be interested in the service of the church in Chanhassen. After obtaining approval from the bishop, Rees moved the church to Eden Prairie on property deeded by Edwin B. Seymour to the wardens and vestrymen of St. John's Episcopal Church in the Wilderness. The property was located in section 27 on the Fort Snelling and Chaska Road (Pioneer Trail) across from what today is the Flying Cloud Airport.

The membership of the church averaged about thirty. Services were conducted by clergy from Excelsior, Shakopee and the Brotherhood of Gethsemane in Minneapolis, with an occasional visit from Bishop H.E. Whipple.

The nearby Methodist and Presbyterian churches were growing and had active youth groups which attracted the young people from St. John's. Some members left to join these congregations. The Brotherhood felt the attendance was now too small to keep going and so the doors were closed. Eventually the church was demolished. Fortunately, pictures remain that tell part of the story of the mission church on the prairie.

Cemeteries

Pleasant Hill Cemetery

From the "Autobiography of Mary Jane Hill Anderson" is the following: "Soon after our arrival in Eden Prairie we experienced our first great sorrow. Our home was on the edge of a meadow near a little creek, which in the spring overflowed. John and little Robert, who were three and five years old, wandered down to the water's edge and fell in. John, somehow, scrambled out by catching hold of the grass on the bank. His cries brought the men, who were home for dinner, but it was too late for little Robert.

"There was no church or graveyard, so we buried little Robert in a field under a tree and marked the place with a rail fence."

On December 27, 1856, in trust for the First Presbyterian Church of Oak Grove, Martin S. McLeon deeded to Gidion H. Pond a three-acre tract of land on the west side of Lyndale Avenue South and 104th Street for a burial ground. This was the first cemetery used by the Eden Prairie Presbyterian Church. It was located a long distance from the church and it was often very difficult to get there. Calvin Anderson remembered his father, John Anderson, telling that it often took two teams of horses to break a trail to the cemetery during the winter months.

This went on until 1885 when the Pleasant Hill Cemetery Association was formed. The association was not in any way affiliated with the church. Land north of the church was purchased from Jacob Wolf. It was a beautiful location overlooking the wide valley to the north with Mill Creek at the base of the hill and Neill Lake in the distance. The first plat contained ninety-six lots. Loved ones were moved from the Bloomington Cemetery to Pleasant Hill.

January was chosen as the month for the annual meeting. At this time officers were elected and all business pertaining to the care of the cemetery was acted upon. Each lot owner was responsible for his lot. There was a general clean-up day twice a year. Lots sold for ten dollars. Money must have been scarce for in 1898 the treasurer reported a balance of $1.41.

One of the association's first expenditures was for fencing the area. The men then planted a row of elm shade trees outside the fence. At the January meeting in 1902 it was moved that these shade trees be cut at the top to a uniform height.

As the years went by, a number of gifts were made to the Cemetery Association. In 1941, under the wise guidance of the church pastor, Rev. James Steenson, who was also a native son, the association purchased Northern States Power stock, which proved to be a very profitable investment and made the association financially sound. Two additional parcels of land have since been purchased: the old church site and one-half acre to the east of it from The Preserve. Now the association provides "perpetual care," but the men still have their spring clean-up day.

This little cemetery back of the church grew into a place of beauty. The leafy branches of the stately elms formed a canopy. One of the fond memories many have of attending the old Presbyterian Church is that in fair weather the people—especially the old—never hurried home from church. They always took a walk in the cemetery. Some stopped at the old pump for a pail of water for the flowers. They never hurried. It was so peaceful that often one had the feeling of being completely in tune with the infinite.

For some it was sad to see the old church go down in 1960 but a deeper tragedy was experienced in 1975 when orange rings were found around most of those stately elms. The leafy branches that once sheltered this sacred ground were now stark naked. The trees had to come down, so the faithful stewards in the association brought their chainsaws and did what had to be done. They planted many trees but many more are still needed.

Eden Prairie Cemetery

The original plat of the Eden Prairie Cemetery Association was surveyed in May, 1864. This beautiful wooded hillside on County Road 4 had been purchased from Alexander Gould. Additional land was purchased in 1906 and 1914 from H.C. and Florence Akeley and from the Eden Prairie Development Company in 1957.

There are no records of cemetery meetings before 1897. On March 9, 1897 new bylaws were adopted and the following officers elected: Frank Rivers, chairman; J.W. Pemberton, secretary; and A.S. Neill, treasurer. The price of a lot (eight graves) at that time was five dollars.

The Eden Prairie Cemetery Association is a non-profit corporation operated by the lot owners who elect three trustees to conduct the business of the association during their three-year terms. An annual meeting is held each year on the last Saturday in April at the cemetery unless otherwise changed at the annual meetings. After the meeting, time is spent in cleaning up the cemetery, visiting, and eating a hearty dinner.

Family names of lot owners on the original plat are Hamilton, Bailey, Schmidel, Apgar, Seiler, Jarrett, Gould, Oothoudt, Good, Seck, Lowell, Fergerson, Smith, Blakely, Staring, Neill, Tuckey, Barker, Miller, Cass, Collins, Cummins, Mitchell, Raguet, Brown, Clark, Moran, Robbins, Rivers, Comstock, Stacy, Tirrell, Paine, Kempton, Gibbs, Hulbert and Pemberton.

Here ends the labors of those who lived before. Their names and epitaphs bring recollections of the past to mind. They contributed much to the history of this community and we respect and honor them in their final resting place.

FARMING

A Humble Beginning

David Livingston, Eden Prairie's first settler, heard the squeak of wheels. Laying down his ax, he walked down the trail a short distance. There in the distance he saw a stranger, with his woman by his side, riding through the tall grass. Two little boys were huddled together in the makeshift wagon behind the slow, plodding team of oxen. A sudden joy embraced David, for here came a man about his age who might help him with two-man jobs and then he'd help him as well.

Famished for company and "woman talk," David's wife, standing at the cabin door, also hoped these folks would settle close by. Oh, if only the first thing in the morning she could see the friendliness of someone's smoke rising over the trees. If only there might be a woman who would come to her in trouble just as she would go to her. One didn't care where the folks came from or how they worshiped God, just so they would settle close by.

"Help yourself to a square of wild paradise," shouted Livingston. "Up to your boot tops the black loam is and there's a creek and lake close by."

John Abbott stopped and stayed longer than he expected while Livingston helped him and his two boys, Hiram and Charles, stake off 160 acres and build a little claim cabin eleven by thirteen feet in size.

Within the next year or two came David Mitchell with his four sons—John, Andrew, Samuel and Alex; Robert and James Anderson, followed later by their mother and six more of her children—Archie, Samuel, William, Sarah, Fannie and Ann Jane; William and Charles Collins; Alexander and Aaron Gould; Richard and William Neill; James and Billy McCoy; the Clark brothers—James, Andrew and John; William, Hugh and Samuel Steenson with their widowed mother; James Gamble; Philander Rouse; Calab Lovering; C.B. Tirrell; John Cummins; William Bryant and Joseph Holasek, to name a few. It wasn't long before all the land in what was to become the township of Eden Prairie was preempted.

These families soon became very close friends. They relied on each other, enjoyed each other and shared their loneliness and homesickness. They were all partners in a strange, yet rich and beautiful land and met their similar situations in as many ways as there were individuals. All suffered the new land's harshness.

Undisturbed through time, grass roots and fibrous creepers had joined with the earth to make a mat which fought obstinately against the sharpest plow and the strongest oxen. One acre a day was all one could expect to turn over. Adding to this drudgery were the buffalo flies, deerflies and those pesky mosquitoes that never stopped buzzing.

There was never an idle moment for there were always log houses and barns to raise, brush to clear, trees to girdle and chop, rail fences to build, big boulders to split with fire and cold water, and always stumps to grub, claw and pry up. When inclement weather prohibited work outdoors, the pioneer made his ax handles and flails, melted lead and made his own bullets, and built crude pieces of furniture for the cabin. Sleep came quickly as he laid his aching muscles on his straw mattress. Survival was all the pioneer could first hope for. Production was too much to expect.

For the housewife there were so many things to do and so little to do them with. One's livelihood was determined by what one got off the land. Her family's diet consisted mainly of potatoes, pork, and cornbread, occasionally varied by fish, venison and other game. In addition, there were the bountiful fruits that unassisted nature yielded in season. Strawberries came in June followed by delicious raspberries and blackberries. There were the grapes that, when preserved in jars of molasses, made delicious pies. Wild plums were as big as eggs. Butternuts were found in favored places while hazelnuts were everywhere. Maple trees yielded quantities of sap for sugar and syrup. An abundance of cranberries was found in the bogs around the area's many lakes.

For the products their families did not consume, these people found a market at the stores and mills in the frontier towns of St. Anthony and St. Paul. Mrs. Robert Anderson told about cranberries selling for one dollar a bushel and how they picked and sold enough to pay for their farm. Joseph Holasek hired his neighbors to pick cranberries. Starting before daybreak he hauled the berries to town in his ox-driven wagon. One season he sold 1,200 bushels of cranberries. The early Eden Prairie families sold wild berries and fruits, maple syrup, and if one found a honey tree there was honey for the market. Wagon loads of potatoes went to town in season. One man told about making brooms from broom corn for the market. Another told about filling his wagon high with straw, which he sold to the St. Anthony ladies who put it under their carpets for warmth or filled mattresses with it. All the cash from these sales was securely locked in the big trunk in the corner of the cabin until the time arrived for them to pay the $1.25 an acre they owed for their land.

The housewife was always at her husband's side in the field. Grain was broadcast by hand. While the farmer cut the grain, his woman bound it by hand. Hay was cut by scythe and carried on peeled poles to the stack. It was a rugged life but the majority were in the prime of early manhood and womanhood. They were in a new country, their surroundings were novel and long life seemed before them. All shared pride in what the land would yield and realized that their longing for independence, prosperity and a farm of their own required a willingness to endure poverty and the fight with the elements.

Panic of 1857

To add to the troubles of these first pioneers, a depression struck in 1857. It was touched off by the failure of the Ohio Loan and Trust Company—a corporation which had been considered as financially sound as the national government itself. At that time most of the money in circulation was in the form of bank bills issued by banks in Ohio, Indiana, Illinois, Wisconsin, Kentucky and Tennessee. Most of these were private banks. Some were wildcat concerns organized to issue currency but were not interested in redeeming it. Banks failed, stores closed and many people went back East. Those who didn't have the money had to stay and get along the best they could.

To add to this forlorn condition of the pioneers, the grasshoppers moved in, eating everything on ground and tree. The pioneers experienced much suffering for the bare necessities of life. It would have been worse had it not been for a market springing up in a most providential manner for a crop which nature planted most generously throughout the woodlands of Hennepin County.

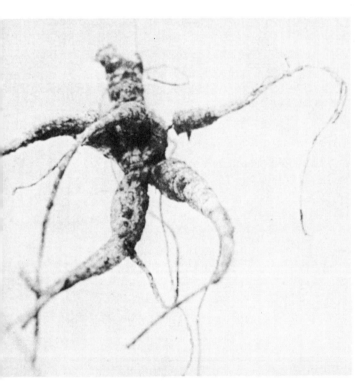

The ginseng root.

Ginseng

Unexpectedly, farmers were given an opportunity to earn some hard cash. In the fall of 1858 several men from an eastern state came and asked people to search for a certain wild plant in the nearby forests. They said they would buy the roots.

This plant was ginseng. The roots were of value because many believed they contained a powerful medicine which could cure fever, weakness and many other ills. People ate the root, made a tonic of it and sometimes crumbled the dry root and smoked it. Ginseng grew wild in the moutain forests of China but now there was not enough to fill the demand.

This plant grew best in cool, damp forests of elm, maple and red oak, which Eden Prairie had in abundance. Every able person took to the woods. The roots weighed but a few ounces each and brought only eight or nine cents a pound. Yet, if a man worked all day he could dig enough to earn three or four dollars. It required no skill and the only equipment needed was a spade or garden hoe. The ginseng trade slowed down after 1859 but it had saved the lives of many pioneers.

Looking up in the 1860s

Farming was now emerging from the survival stage into the production stage. The Indian Outbreak of 1862 and the Civil War brought great hardships but now the farmers seemed to have the land under their control with large fields devoted to one single crop, wheat. Improved milling methods had provided an expanding market for wheat in the 1860s. In his "History of Hennepin County," Dr. Edward Neill wrote that more grain was shipped out of Hennepin Landing in Eden Prairie than any other place in the county. This put money in the farmer's pockets. Four little general stores, Rowland, Rankins, Goodrich and Tuckey, opened up to meet the ever-increasing material demands of the town. A little flour mill was built on Mill Creek. The pioneers had just gained a feeling of prosperity when tragedy struck again.

91

Grasshoppers were collected by some of the settlers who collected bounties on their catch. From Frank Leslie's Illustrated Newspapers, September 1, 1888; Courtesy Library of Congress, Minnesota Historical Society.

The Grasshoppers of 1873

It happened around June 12, 1873 when a breeze from the Southwest guided hordes of Rocky Mountain locusts into Minnesota. The insect army caught farmers by surprise. One man who had been working in his garden took off his vest. "Suddenly," he said, "my attention was attached to the sky and I never saw a more beautiful sight. A horde of grasshoppers were alighting. Nothing was more beautiful than the shimmering of the sun on their thousands of gold-bronze wings could be imagined. They took everything and then passed on leaving the garden looking as if it had been burned. When I went for my vest, they had eaten it all but the seams."

Some said the winged invaders made the sound like roaring wind or like a prairie fire. No open door or windows were safe from intrusion. They clustered around buildings and swarmed over people's shoes, eating the laces. Trains were delayed while grasshoppers were shoveled from the track. Farmers turned the soil that fall, hoping the frost would kill them. But in 1874 the eggs hatched and new plantings were completely destroyed. Bounties were offered for dead 'hoppers. Tar-covered iron plates were dragged across infested fields. Hay was spread and burned to cremate the insects. Henry Tuckey said that the farmers in Eden Prairie pitched them into wagons and dumped them over the Shakopee hill. You could smell them for a mile.

In the spring of 1877, four years after the grasshoppers' arrival, Governor Pillsbury decided in desperation to try other means of ridding the state of grasshoppers. He announced a statewide day of prayer and fasting. The people filled the churches and

92

prayed aloud to God. Then something unexplainable happened. Instead of flying from field to field laying eggs, the 'hoppers flew up and out of the state. That night a hard freeze killed the eggs. By the middle of August Minnesota was free of grasshoppers and the state farmers were busy harvesting the largest wheat crop in history.

Better Years Ahead

The pioneers, who had the courage to survive repeated setbacks that came through no fault of their own, were now facing the future with new hope. The log-cabin babies, now of age, were ready to take over. Some stayed on the home place while others bought farms nearby.

Planting wheat year after year had drained the soil of valuable nutrients, causing production to decrease. As wheat profits declined, the farmers turned to new crops such as corn, oats, barley, flax and alfalfa. More land was put under cultivation with the advent of new machinery such as the sulky and gang plows, harrows, riding cultivators, corn planters, grain binders and mowers, to name a few.

Attention was now focused on dairy cows, hogs, chickens and garden marketing. The windmill had replaced the hand pump. The incubator and brooder house replaced the setting hen. Through experiments in selecting and grafting, apples, grapes, plums and raspberries that could withstand the cold Minnesota winters were developed. Now almost every farm had its orchard, vineyard and berry patch.

The Grange

In 1849 Oliver Hudson Kelly took up a claim near Elk River. He suffered all the trials and frustrations of an early pioneer. He had always felt the need for an organization in which the farmers could work together and improve their lives.

In 1867 Kelly went to Washington to work in the Post Office Department. While in Washington a small group of men and women became interested in his idea, which resulted in the organization of the National Grange of the Patrons of Husbandry.

The first purposes of the Grange were to help educate the farmers and their families and to enrich their social lives. Other purposes of the Grange were to help farmers get the latest information on marketing crops and livestock and the availability of new farm machinery; to set up places in cities where farm produce could be sold; and to protect the farmer against exploitation, whether it be the railroads or the middle man with whom he had to deal.

The Eden Prairie Grange, founded October 22, 1873, was among the first organized in the state. Meetings were held at the Goodrich Hall above the Goodrich Store on Pioneer Trail. One of the important men in each local and state Grange was the lecturer. He prepared the programs for each meeting. This organization had a great influence on the progressive farming methods in the township.

Eden Prairie Grange No. 366; organized October 22, 1873.

It wasn't long before the mailman began bringing magazines such as the "Farm Journal," "The Farmer," "The Country Gentleman," as well as bulletins from the University of Minnesota Extension Division. Also, arriving in the spring and fall was the Sears and Roebuck catalog with its pages of tantalizing new equipment for farm and home.

Huge barns were now built with immense care as they were the measures of the size of a farmer's dream. Great efforts were made to improve the quality of country living. The log cabins were replaced by large frame houses with rambling porches. Hanging kerosene lamps with decorative shades, floral patterned carpets and a new organ in the parlor were the housewife's pride. After years of rubbing clothes on a washboard, knuckles raw and aching and arms lame from wringing heavy clothes by hand, the housewife raised her head in thanks to the men who invented the clothes wringer and then the washing machine.

The somewhat liberated lady of the house now hitched her spirited little horse to the family buggy and took off for the Ladies Aid meeting, a quilting bee, or maybe a homemaking class by the University of Minnesota Extension Division. There was time now to become involved in the community's education program. Parents attended the annual school meetings where the qualifications of teachers and textbooks were discussed. The spelling bees, school exhibits, plays and speaking contests were now special events.

Calico Ball

One special event that held the attention of many for a number of years was the Calico Ball, held the last part of May at the Goodrich Hall.

The ladies put great thought and time into making their neat little print dresses with full skirts and trimmed in lace and pretty buttons. Many a young maid dreamed of

Invitation to the Calico Ball at the Goodrich Hall.

romance as she stitched and sewed. It was spring, lilac time, when a young man's fancy turns to love.

The Calico Ball was a happy occasion. They danced, they laughed, they visited. There were flirtations of all degrees of seriousness. There were the scheming mamas maneuvering daughters into paths of youths with prospects. When not twirling their partners, the fathers were deeply engrossed in talk about the prospects for that year's crop. Grandmas and grandpas sat in their chairs along the side of the room and seemed pleased as they looked on at this second generation.

The Automobile

If one were to pick a time of the most noticeable change in Eden Prairie it would have to be around 1915 when the Ford, Velie, Star, Essex, Overland, Studebaker and Nash cars showed up in the farmers' yards and brought with them increased social mobility. Business contacts were vastly enlarged by this new rapid means of travel and a new era of farm marketing began. This change would have proceeded more rapidly

Andrew Glenn home on County Road 18; summer 1893.

if it hadn't been for World War I and the shortage of labor it caused, the collapse of farm prices in the 1920s followed by the drought and the Depression of the 1930s. It took the years of World War II and the Korean War to restore not only the economy, but farmers' confidence.

Now the great storehouse of scientific technology delayed by depression and wars made possible entirely new methods of agricultural production which resulted in higher yields through the use of improved plant and animal strains, fertilizers and pesticides, and especially sophisticated farm equipment. More pounds of meat or milk from less feed became the focus of breeding efforts. Soybeans became a new cash crop in the 1930s and increased in importance until it ranked next to corn in production in the 1950s. Some of this new scientific approach

was brought to Eden Prairie's front door when the Northrup King Company in 1934 purchased a large tract of land in central Eden Prairie for their seed research center.

Although there were fewer farmers in Eden Prairie, there was more land in production. The rich green alfalfa and golden oat and corn fields were being turned into milk and butter. It was a simplified task for one farmer to operate a number of farms with his two or three tractors with equipment of like size. Barns were made larger and mechanized to accommodate the larger dairy herds. The well-educated third-generation farmer kept close records, for in order to succeed now one had to know how to increase production and cut costs.

Suddenly in the 1960s a change took place. All that had been built up was swept away.

Horace Goodrich home on Pioneer Trail; built in early 1880s.

Home of James Gamble, Edward Gamble, and the Elmer Clark family (Bertha Gamble). Built in the 1880s.

Just when larger farms were needed to function economically, the price of land skyrocketed and real-estate taxes climbed to unprecedented heights. Increased costs of feed and dairy equipment put the squeeze on. Economically, the farmer could not maintain his former way of life. Lured by the high prices for land, he signed his life's heritage away to the new man on the scene: the land developer.

Raspberries

In the spring of 1879 Joe and John Empanger went to Minneapolis with their supply of butter and eggs. On the way, they stopped in St. Louis Park to visit George Pratt while they rested their oxen. Naturally the conversation turned to the conditions of the markets and the price of farm produce. Mr. Pratt laughed and said, "I've something that will really bring money in time." He showed them a patch of Philadelphia raspberries, then gave them some plants to plant on their farms. That was the beginning of experimentation in the Hopkins area to find the best ways to raise the most marketable raspberry which at the same time would withstand the cold Minnesota winters. When the State Fruit Breeding Farm was established, the work of developing and introducing new varieties was carried on at the fruit farm.

It wasn't long before the raspberries from Minnetonka, Hopkins and northern Eden Prairie were being shipped from coast to coast. They were sold at roadside stands, chain stores, food markets of all types and in the large public markets of Minneapolis and St. Paul. After the Excelsior Cooperative Fruit Growers Association was formed, berries were sent from there and its substation in Hopkins by truck and railway over an area that covered five states. In the 1930 season ninety-six carloads—around eighty thousand crates—were shipped out of Excelsior and Hopkins. Multiply that by twenty-four pints and you get close to two million boxes, which represent many backaches for the hot, tired berry pickers.

In 1935 Hopkins celebrated its first midsummer Raspberry Festival with a mile-long parade, beautiful girls competing for the honor of Raspberry Queen, and special programs with music, speakers and contests. Free bowls of raspberries were given to everyone. This festival is still held today but one will find few berries given away. Those that are have been frozen and shipped from elsewhere.

The rich, green raspberry bushes covering the hills of northern Eden Prairie are now gone. Sons did not replace their fathers on the berry farms. The temptation of a new land boom with berry patches being platted into home sites ended the era of berry farming. Only a few now hold in their memories this special beauty of northern Eden Prairie.

Dairying in Eden Prairie

The dairy cow was the backbone of the early farmer's income. In the form of homemade butter, the settlers were provided with a ready method of securing a small amount of cash. As more cows were added, the income from dairy products was usually the money that paid the taxes. From this small beginning grew the gigantic dairy industry of Hennepin County. Some of the developments and inventions which occurred since the 1850s are startling: the silo, the cream separator, the rotary churn, the milking parlors, pasteurized and bottled milk, and scientific feeding and breeding for production.

This large industry was not developed without severe growing pains. At first, making butter and cheese was the farmwife's work. It was she who generally took her produce to the general store and traded it for groceries. Often it was hard for the local merchants to accept some of this butter and cheese for the quality varied as widely as the housewives' standards of housekeeping.

In the 1890s a little creamery opened across from the Miller Brothers store by the railroad tracks on County Road 4. The cream-

1907 Thrashing machine. Hank Kutcher and Frank Seck.

Nelson Mitchell on a horse drawn grain binder.

Feeding chickens on the Tuckey farm.

ery served the farmers as an outlet for their milk and cream until it closed around 1902. After the creamery closed, some farmers got together and shipped their milk by train, each taking a turn going to town with the milk cans. Others had the tiresome and tedious job of hauling the milk to customers in the city. Farmers in a neighborhood would band together for the hauling, each taking his turn. One farmer said that the milk dealers had two complaints: the milk was often frozen in the winter and frequently soured before delivery during the summer months. Mrs. Howard Good remembered when the farmers would haul the milk on a cart out to the main road. There it would sit in all kinds of weather until it was picked up—sometimes getting to town late at night.

In 1915 the farmers were receiving a low price—nine cents a gallon—for milk with no attention to butterfat, quality or cleanliness. Hennepin County agent K.A. Kirkpatrick called a meeting on March 1, 1916 for the purpose of discussing and ironing out the milk problems. At this meeting he proposed the organization of the Twin City Milk Producers Association. To make a go of this association, 2,500 farmers had to sign up. A committee was selected to help Kirkpatrick obtain members. Through their efforts the 2,500 farmers signed up before September of that year. It wasn't long before ninety percent of all fluid milk sold in the Twin Cities and suburbs was supplied by this organization. During periods when there was a surplus the milk was manufactured into butter, cheese, dried milk and other dairy products.

Now large dairy farms dotted the prairie with herds of fifty and more in size. Farmers took pride in their herds and without a doubt there was a certain degree of competition among them as to production and butterfat count. Some of the big herds were those of the Nesbitt brothers, Ralph and Stanley; the Anderson brothers, Kenneth and Calvin; the Miller brothers, Arthur and Fred; Loring Tuckey; Dana Pemberton; Sheldon Douglas; Roland Rogers; Alfred

Blakeborough; Emil Pauly; and William and Lorman Jarrett. Frank Griswald bought property near Anderson Lakes, where The Preserve is today, and called it Franlo Farms. His registered Holsteins won national and international fame in production and showmanship.

Today consumers never give quality of milk a thought but take it for granted. The milk is produced under sanitary conditions, rigidly inspected and sold on a quality and butterfat basis. Much credit for the organization of this method of handling milk must go to the dynamic K.A. Kirkpatrick and his work as Hennepin County agent for more than twenty-five years. It is he who organized the first 4-H Club in Eden Prairie, the cattle-judging teams, and encouraged the young boys to further their farm education after graduation from high school.

Hennepin County Fair

The Hennepin County Agricultural Society has a long history. It was formed February 26, 1853 with the first fair held October 20 of the same year. Although the location is vague, it was probably in the area opposite the Nicollet Hotel on Washington Avenue in Minneapolis. An interesting item at that fair and one which attracted the most interest was an exhibit of three apples by Gideon Pond. For a time the fair was discontinued. Then, in 1907, the Hopkins Commercial Club decided to hold a harvest festival and solicited funds on Main Street for that purpose. Much to their surprise, they had ample funds.

Exhibits were in the local halls, livestock were housed in large tents, and concessions were on the main street. The charge for viewing the exhibits was five cents. To the surprise of the managers, they even made a little profit.

This arrangement continued for several years when finally the organization bought a piece of land south of Exelsior Avenue between 13th and 17th streets for a fair-

Modern machinery on the Sever Peterson farms. Located on the way to Shakopee on Flying Cloud Drive.

Edwin Phipps Asparagus Truck, 1918.

Hauling milk to the Twin City Milk Producer's Creamery in the 1920s.

Making hay in 1915.

Haystack mover. Al Hjorth on the Rowland Ridge farm in the 1950s.

Eden Prairie Creamery located across from the Miller Brothers Store by the railroad tracks; about 1900.

ground. Livestock, poultry, and exhibit buildings were constructed. There was a half-mile race track and a viewing stand.

From this small beginning grew one of the most progressive county fairs in the state, a fair that attracted livestock from herds with national and international reputations. This, too, came to an end in the 1960s with the change from country to suburban living. The grounds were purchased by the City of Hopkins.

The 4-H Club

I pledge—
My Head for clearer thinking,
My Heart to greater loyalty,
My Hands to larger service,
My Health to better living,
for
My Home, my Club, my Community, and my Country.

The 4-H Club is the youth education program of the Agricultural Extension Service of the University of Minnesota and is conducted in cooperation with the County Extension Service and the United States Department of Agriculture.

Its objective is to help boys and girls between the ages of nine and nineteen to accept responsibilities and leadership through practical experience in day-to-day living. The 4-H projects are the basis of this educational program. Members learn by doing. Projects are done in the home and on the farm under the guidance of parents, local 4-H Club leaders, and junior leaders—members with a number of years experience.

The 4-H clubs began in 1914. Hennepin County agent K.A. Kirkpatrick organized 4-H in Eden Prairie. At that time, emphasis was on dairy herd improvement in cooperation with the South Hennepin Herd Improvement Association. Through his leadership and the help of interested parents, a number of Eden Prairie boys received state and national recognition for their excellence in management and cattle judging.

Some of the local 4-H Club leaders of the past are Mrs. Ben Anderson, Mrs. Charles Hulbert, Mrs. Lorman Jarrett, Mrs. Howard Good, Kenneth Anderson, Mrs. Harland Bohland, Mr. and Mrs. Ralph Nesbitt, Mrs. John Bren and Mrs. Daniel Totushek.

MEMORIES OF THE FARM

Threshing

The thought of threshing time brings fond memories. I remember in the days of the steam engine my sister, brother and I would climb to the highest window in the house and wait for the smoke of the engine to appear over the hill and listen for the sound of its whistle as it drew near the farmyard.

Margaret Picha Bren

Threshing time was fun. Four-horse binders were used to harvest the grain. The bundles of grain were set up in shocks, then later hauled to a central area of the field where cone-shaped stacks were built. There were few rigs around at that time so farmers had to wait their turn. Sometimes there was snow on the ground. Phillips from Excelsior, with his big steam engine, took care of our area.

I was only seven years old when I first helped my aunt at threshing time. Phillips had a crew of six men. They slept in the barn. It was some job to feed those guys breakfast, dinner, supper, and lunch in between. If it rained they'd hang around until they could work again.

Each farmer had to furnish wood for the engine. If they ran out of wood they'd burn fence posts or straw. One man was on the water wagon. He'd fill up barrels from some nearby lake or creek and line them up near the engine and go back for more. There was always a man on the stack and one to sack grain. I remember the long black belt that ran from the separator to the engine. They had to watch out for fire. The engine whistle blew the signals: one whistle, out of water; two whistles, out of sack; three whistles, time to eat.

The men washed under the big shade tree in the backyard where a basin, towel, soap, and a ten-gallon cream can of rain water from the cistern was provided. Then they filed into the kitchen. I sure know what it means to "eat like a harvest hand."

We had to get up early to get those big threshing meals ready. Pies were baked and placed on the pantry shelf. Loaves of bread were set to rise before going into the oven. There was always a big roast with lots of gravy, mountains of mashed potatoes, many kinds of garden vegetables, plus jams, jellies and pickles. Often the women in the neighborhood competed with each other to see who could put out the best meal.

After a short nap under the shade trees it was back to work again for the men. For the women, it was soon lunch time again. Out to the field we went with meat-filled sandwiches, cake, doughnuts, cookies, and the big black pot full of hot coffee.

I remember when my older brother, Alfred, bought an Almond tractor with big steel wheels. The Kopesky and Perkl boys, along with Shorty Palmer, used to help him. Loring Tuckey used to run the separator.

Later there were other farmers with tractors and threshing machines. Some were Emil Dvorak, Calvin Anderson, the Nesbitt brothers, the Miller brothers, Roland Rogers and Alvin Holasek. Now they didn't stack the grain and just a few close neighbors worked together.

No matter how tired the men got at threshing time, there was always a lot of teasing, joking and laughing. If there was a breakdown they all pitched in.

I think the Nesbitts were the only ones to try combining grain. By that time there wasn't much farming in Eden Prairie.

Priscilla Blakeborough Good

Butchering

We raised our own hogs and saw to it that they were properly fed on cracked corn, oats, and separated milk or buttermilk. The best hogs weighed from 150 to 200 pounds and were from twelve to eighteen months old.

We usually butchered three or four hogs at a time for we had a big family, a hired girl and sometimes a hired man. Some folks butchered by the sign of the moon but we never bothered about that.

There was lots of excitement on butchering day. The neighbors came to help. We had a good time. My dad had to get up early to get the fire going under the big black pot for the water had to be at least 180 degrees F. in order to scald the hogs to the point that the hair would come off.

First we killed the hogs and then saw that they were well bled. The men would put a big hook in the hog's head. Hot water was put in a big barrel and the men would keep pulling the hog up and down and turning him around. When the hog was clean of hair it was hung from the rafters in a nearby shed.

Next came the cleaning. Here is where the women came in with their tubs and buckets for the heart, liver, tongue, head, and other parts used in making sausage and head cheese. The intestines were cleaned and used for casings for the sausage. We'd let the hogs hang for a day until all the animal heat was gone.

Now came the important part: cutting up the hogs into hams and bacon, trimming them close, for the trimmings were worth more made into sausage and lard than left on the hams and bacon. We'd use about one pound of salt peter for one hundred pounds of meat. This was rubbed in the meat and around the bones. One could add a pound of sugar to each twenty pounds of salt if he liked. Now the meat was placed on a long board for about a week, resalted and then cured again for another four or five weeks, depending on the size of the hams and bacon. The salt was rubbed off and the surface was rubbed with red and black pepper. Now they were ready to be hung in the smokehouse.

My dad, Henry Pauly, was known to turn out the best ham and bacon in the neighborhood. He was very fussy about the smoking process. The fire was started with corncobs and then he'd pile on hickory sticks. He kept a close watch on that fire to see the smoke was just right and also that no fat drippings would fall on the fire and start flames which could spoil the hams and bacon. Hams and bacon were smoked for about two weeks while sausage took just about two days.

After the hams and bacon were taken out of the smokehouse they were soaked in a lime bath to exclude insects and preserve the color and flavor. Now they were ready to be hung up again in the darkest part of the smokehouse or down in the cellar. Sometimes we'd put them in a tight barrel and bury them in the oats bin.

Sausage grinding was a family affair, for we all worked at it. The grinding machine was nailed to a six-foot board, which was placed between two chairs. It had dozens of sharp blades and was operated by a crank. Mother could make the best sausage and head cheese. The neighborhood women always asked her to help them. Sometimes she'd fry down pork, put it in a crock jar and pour lard on top. That sealed it so well that it kept until the next butchering.

I'll tell you, those hams and bacons were good and came in handy on the farm. When company came to the house, Mother would run out to the smokehouse or down into the cellar for meat. It didn't take long before we were all at the table eating a meal fit for a king.

Emil Pauly

Feather-Stripping Bees

I've lived on this farm sixty-one years. My husband, Edward, would be ninety his next birthday if he were living. He was born in that room just off this dining room. His parents, Frank and Josephine, owned many acres in this Duck Lake area. Now houses cover all this land. All I have left is one acre. But the people who have built houses are good neighbors. They are so good to me.

I know about feather-stripping bees, for we raised ducks and geese. About in late August or September, just before we started to fatten them for butchering, we'd catch the birds and strip off their breast feathers. They surely looked funny running around without their feathers. We'd store the feathers in gunny sacks until the winter months.

At butchering time we'd take off the rest of the feathers. The wings were saved, for they were good for dusting furniture and getting cobwebs out of corners. The big feathers were tied together and used for greasing pans. We saved and stored all the goose grease in crocks for cooking. Goose grease was considered the best remedy for chest colds. Our mothers would just rub the hot grease on our chest or sometimes mix it with camphor oil. It was a sure cure.

The feather-stripping bees were held in the winter. We'd invite all the neighbor women. My mother cooked lots of food and the women brought lots of food and stayed all day. They sat around the big kitchen table and ripped the soft down feathers from the ribs, making sure they got only the best feathers. They'd laugh, sing, tell stories and tell jokes on each other. They'd take time out to eat, go back to stripping for a while and then back to eating again. The feathers flew all over.

These feathers were stored in sacks until there was time to make pillows and the feather ticks that kept us so cozy and warm during the cold winter months. Ever so often, we'd take the feather ticks outside and shake them well so as to get the feathers evenly distributed again.

Mrs. Edward (Frances) Jerabek

Sauerkraut

Yes, I helped make sauerkraut. We made only enough for our family. There was a large oak barrel down in the cellar. The men would strip the large outer leaves off the cabbage in the field and then bring them into the kitchen where the cabbage cutter was set up.

We'd carry the shredded cabbage down to the cellar. First we put in a layer of cabbage, then salt, and maybe some caraway seed. We'd keep adding cabbage and salt. A big stomper was used to press down the cabbage. Sometimes we used our feet. I remember many times jumping into the kraut barrel and stomping down the cabbage. When the barrel was full, it was sealed until the kraut was ready to eat.

Mrs. Edward (Frances) Jerabek

Berry Picking

It's hard to believe that where Rosemount, Inc., is today there used to be big raspberry patches. John Tobias, my Dad, owned that farm. It was sold to Rosemount in 1965.

My memories of raising raspberries are that it was one tough job. We'd cultivate the patches with a horse and hand cultivator. I suppose they use garden tractors today. My Dad would send my brothers—Edward and Clarence—and me out to hoe. It was hoe, hoe, hoe all day long. We sure hated that job. After fruiting, all the old prickly canes had to be cut out. In the fall the bushes had to be bent over and covered with dirt to prevent winter kill.

The Latham, or Big Four, was a good berry, a little later than the early Kings, but it bore fruit for a longer time. When the berries were ripe all the neighbor kids came to pick berries. It was the only job available for kids in those days. I think for a time they got about seventy cents for picking a crate. We got our crates from the Bren Box Factory on Shady Oak Road. I think for a time they only cost twenty-three cents a crate, but then we were only getting about $1.25 a crate for berries. My dad got up at four o'clock in the morning and took the berries to the Minneapolis Market on First Avenue North. There the merchants were waiting and eager to buy the berries.

Joe Viska had one of the largest berry farms located on County Road 18. His farm is now part of Anderson Lakes Park.

There were berry patches all over the northern part of Eden Prairie. John Pobuda had a large berry farm where Sears store is today. Some of the berry pickers came from Silver

Lake and Hutchinson. They were either relatives or friends of the Czechs in Eden Prairie. They boarded and roomed at the farms. After working hours these young people had lots of fun. Many romances started during berry picking time. Ask some of the old timers how they met their wives and many will answer, "In the berry patch."

After Highway 169 was built many of the farmers opened fruit and vegetable stands along the highway. Starting from the north, there were the Bill and Dick Kopesky stands. Alvin Bren had a stand at the junction of Shady Oak Road and Highway 169. By the Wye was Sam Watkins' stand and farther down was Claude Buckingham's stand. On the corner of Sunnybrook Road was the big Jack Raguet Sunnybrook Market. On the top of Shakopee hill, Martin Grill operated the Vegetable Grill. I guess that's still in operation.

Folks from the city made weekly trips out to the country stands. They came back year after year. These were the days when housewives canned lots of fruits and vegetables. Now with our big supermarkets with fresh fruits available all year around there is no need for these stands. Then with the fast cars and people racing to get from here to there, no one can take the time to enjoy these roadside stands.

Elmer Tobias

Marketing

Eden Prairie farmers got up at midnight for the long trip to Minneapolis. Wagons loaded with vegetables moved slowly along the winding dirt roads. At first these wagons were drawn by oxen and then later by horses. Many farmers sold their vegetables from house to house. In the fall some housewives bought enough potatoes to last through the winter.

As the demand for fresh fruits and vegetables increased, the farmers felt there was a need for a central marketplace. In 1871

Harlow Gale opened the first farmers market on First Street and Bridge Square (near the first span bridge of Minneapolis). Many farmers were now happy that they no longer had to sell their produce at curbsides along the streets. By 1890, this market had outgrown its building and location. T.B. Walker put up the money to finance construction of a larger market at Sixth Street and Second Avenue that could serve around three hundred gardeners. It cost twenty-five cents for a stall or $7.50 for the season. This location soon became too congested and the farmers, who had now organized the Minneapolis Producers Association, felt the need for a new location and proposed a city-owned market be built at Lyndale and Glenwood Avenue. This market opened in 1938 with over 1,200 growers using the market. The Market Producers Association ran the market with a marketmaster in charge. Alvin Bren of Eden Prairie is the present marketmaster.

This market was a very busy place with gardeners from Osseo, Brooklyn Center, Minnetonka, Bloomington and Eden Prairie bringing in fresh produce each day. Some of the growers from Eden Prairie were the Brens, Kopeskys, Uherkas, Viskas, Holaseks, John Tobias, Dean Oothoudt, Edwin Phipps, Ernest Hone, John Raguet and Sever Peterson. They sold their produce to the local grocers who came to market each morning as well as to the people who enjoyed that early-morning trip to the market.

Business slowed down in the Fifties when the housewives started using canned and frozen fruits and vegetables. When big supermarkets sprang up around the city some farmers started selling direct to these big stores. Yet, the market has remained a fairly busy place as it's still a great gathering place for some grocers and people who enjoy going to market and visiting with farmers and friends while selecting choice fruits and vegetables.

One thing we vegetable gardeners learned was thrift, for the money we took in during the harvest season had to last until the next year's crop was harvested.

John Bren

Making Wood

Many people settled in Eden Prairie because it had two attractive features: wood and water. It is hard for us today to visualize that dense woods of sturdy oak covered the greater part of the town. For years wood was the only source of heat and the big woodpile behind the house symbolized security and warmth.

Making wood came in the winter months. It was plenty cold when we took off with our axes and saws. We'd either chop or saw down the big trees, trim off the branches, and then with two-man saws cut the trees into sixteen-foot logs. For two men to make the crosscut go smoothly required a close coordination of push, pull and pressure. When it goes well it's fairly pleasant work. If the wood were close to the house the logs were piled right there. Otherwise, they were hauled home by sled and piled near the house.

Some farmers had their own saw rigs but most of them depended on the man who traveled from farm to farm sawing wood.

The first saw rigs were powered by hit-and-miss gas engines. These engines were mounted on a heavy, iron-wheeled wagon and moved from place to place with a team of horses. These saw rigs had large flywheels about four feet in diameter. The engine huffed away quietly until the saw teeth hit the log. Then a few quick explosions speeded up the blade and cut the log in two. When one pile of logs was cut up, the rig moved ahead and tackled another pile. When old cars became available some men mounted their rigs on a platform behind the motor. Then came the tractor with the long heavy belt running from tractor to saw rig.

There was no time for play after school. We'd come home, have a quick lunch, and then go to our first chore of filling the woodbox by the kitchen stove. We'd pile our arms full of sticks. It was back and forth from the woodpile to the house. Growing boys detested this job but it did develop muscles.

Albert Picha

Harvesting Ice

Keeping food from spoiling has always been a problem. The pioneer women used the lakes and streams and later the cellar beneath their houses. The invention of the icebox called for cakes of ice. Many farmers built ice houses and insulated them with sawdust and wood chips. They harvested ice on nearby lakes, hauled it home and packed it in the ice houses with layers of sawdust between the cakes.

Clean ice was needed for the homes in the city and also for the growing railroad system with its newly invented refrigerated boxcars. To meet this need the Cedar Lake Ice Company was founded in 1878 in Minneapolis. Ice was harvested from Cedar Lake. But the city did not like ice houses for they felt the sawdust was a fire hazard.

The company then built a big ice house on Riley's Lake in Eden Prairie. It was sixty by two hundred feet in size and four stories high. The exterior had double walls. The interior was divided into double walled sections. Sawdust was poured in between these double walls. This ice house was located just down the hill and across the tracks from the Howard Good home. Howard remembers the days of harvesting ice.

"The third story of our house was made into a bunkhouse. There was an outside stairway that led up to this third story. We boarded up to forty men at a time. Our neighbors, the Dorns, and Bill Sass also boarded some men.

The ice was usually harvested late in December and January. By February it started to honeycomb. When the lake froze to a depth of sixteen to twenty inches teams of horses were brought to the lake. They were hitched to ten-foot-wide snow scrapers which removed the snow to the shore. Next a baseline, which had to be perfectly straight, was scored on the ice by a horse-drawn plow knife. Parallel cuts were then made twenty-eight inches from the baseline and twenty-eight inches apart until the ice field was scored.

A channel was made to the ice house. The ice blocks were guided into this channel and then up into the building on a conveyor system called a "gallery." It consisted of heavy, endless chains with hooks and iron separator bars attached to them for gripping the ice blocks. This was operated by a big gasoline engine. Along the front of the building were platforms where the men stood and guided the ice blocks from the conveyor and distributed them in the big rooms. All sections of ice were heavily covered with sawdust.

In the summer some of the crew came back. They loaded the ice into railroad cars that carried the ice into the city.

This ice house burned in 1912. The next year, the Cedar Lake Ice Company built an ice house on Shady Oak Lake west of Hopkins. It was so big some say it covered an acre of land. It was the biggest storage house west of Chicago. Some men from Eden Prairie worked there. They got five dollars a day, which was big pay in those days, but there was little profit for they had to spend so much for warm clothes. With the temperature getting down to thirty degrees below zero and a forty-mile wind blowing across that lake it took a lot of clothes to keep warm.

Howard Good

Brown's Goat Farm

This farm was located across from the water plant on Mitchell Road. My great grandmother, Ann Jane Anderson Brown, purchased this land in section sixteen from the United States Government. The government had designated that money received from the sale of land in section sixteen be used for school purposes.

My grandfather was James Brown. His brother, George, who was a bachelor, lived on this farm until his death. To settle the estate, my father, Truman, and his brother, Arthur, bought the farm. Neither men were farmers. My father had been superintendent of a number of schools in Minnesota and Arthur was a professor at Stout University in Wisconsin.

The farm had a fine dairy herd with all the milk delivered to the Glen Lake Sanitarium. But there was one problem. The place was overrun by rats. My uncle had read someplace that billy goats would get rid of rats so they purchased a small herd of goats in Wisconsin. Soon the men started reading up on the raising of goats and the production of goat milk. More goats were purchased. The dairy herd was sold and the barns remodeled with stanchions placed on platforms for easier milking. A milk route was started in the cities. To acquaint people with the taste of goat's milk a booth was set up at the state fair where they handed out samples of goat milk.

Then in 1943 a man from the Veterans Hospitals in Maryland came by and said he needed a herd of five hundred goats. They sold the whole herd plus some they rounded up to make the five hundred. My dad and his brother then split up, as my father had all he could do to run his father's farm on Riverview Road.

Uncle Arthur built up a new herd, discontinued the milk route, and hired a Swiss couple who devoted all their time to making cheese and powdered milk. This went on until my uncle's death in the 1950's.

People from all over the country who were interested in goats visited the farm. I remember Carl Sandburg, the poet and author, and Burl Ives, the folk singer, both visited the farm while visiting in Minneapolis.

In 1950 the New York production of "Mr. Roberts" with Henry Fonda played at the Lyceum Theater. The play called for a goat and the manager was directed to our farm in Eden Prairie. The goat they picked had to be brought into town for each performance.

I remember standing backstage holding onto that goat. It was exciting to witness the activities backstage.

James Brown

ORGANIZATIONS

The Farmers Club

This was the most active club in Eden Prairie for many years. It had ninety-four members at one time.

I remember going to the meetings with my parents when the meetings were held in the Anderson and Wolf schools. After these schools were closed the club met in the basement of the Presbyterian Church. The club gave the church gas for the lamps and cordwood for the use of the basement. I think the children liked the good lunches—delicious sandwiches, doughnuts, cake and cocoa. Sometimes we were asked to take part in the programs.

The programs were usually put on by the club members. They started with vocal and piano solos, humorous readings, recitations, pantomimes and one-act plays. The main program followed. There were talks by club members; our county agent, Mr. Kirkpatrick; Charles Hulbert of Eden Prairie, our state representative; and other guest speakers who talked on subjects of interest to farmers. Often the club had debates with neighboring clubs. Looking through an old secretary's book, I found some of the topics for debate were: "Resolve that vegetable gardening is more profitable than dairying," "Should farmers be permitted to use chemical sprays," "House doctors versus patent medicines," "Should manufacturers be permitted to color oleomargarine," "Are chain stores good or bad." A number of programs were on trying to get electricity in Eden Prairie.

Some club members were leaders for the young people's sewing club, chicken club and calf club, and helped put on an achievement day each year.

In the winter there was an oyster supper and in the summer a July 4 picnic. There were ice-cream socials and basket socials. At a basket social each lady brought a basket lunch. Some were really very fancy. The baskets were auctioned off and the highest bidder got to eat with the girl who brought the basket. One time Amos Anderson wanted a certain girl's basket. The fellows knew it and kept bidding until Amos had to pay eighteen dollars for the basket. That was a lot money in those days.

But the biggest project of the year was the booth for the county fair. Many weeks were spent on this exhibit booth. The club was divided into committees on corn, vegetables, fresh fruits, canning, grain, grasses and miscellaneous items. We won many county and state prizes on our booth and exhibits. The clubs in the county put on stunts at the fair. We came out first many times.

One big benefit club members had was that they could buy items cooperatively and get them at greatly reduced prices. Carloads of coal and cattle salt were bought and placed on the side tracks by the depot. Each farmer had to weigh what he got on the scales at Miller's store. The club also took orders for fly spray, rope, alcohol (distillate), and many kinds of seeds. An old secretary's book showed orders were taken for household items. One order was for 115 pounds of coffee, nine boxes of soap, 825 pounds of sugar and 350 pounds of flour. The complete order came to $142.15. It's a bit shocking when one compares this with today's prices.

Beatrice Glenn Veness

Ward Holasek and Hennepin County Agent George Roadfeldt.

First prize booth at the Hennepin County Fair, 1950s

Eden Prairie Eagles 4-H Club

The years spent as 4-H Club leaders were the happiest times on the farm. We had an enthusiastic group of boys and girls to work with and parents who were behind them all the way. Without this the club could never have achieved the many awards won on the county, state and national levels.

Each member had to pick a project. In Eden Prairie it was mostly diary cattle, gardening, cooking and dressmaking. Definite instructions had to be followed and detailed reports filled out before a project could be entered at the county fair. Two projects the group worked on as a whole were health and good grooming.

Mary Ellen Anderson with her 4-H Club heifer "7 Up".

4-H Club calf judging at the Hennepin County Fair in the 1950s.

The 4-H Club in the Hopkins Raspberry Parade in the 1950s.

The club met in the homes of the members once a month. Because of their good-grooming project the boys and girls always came looking their best. The officers of the club took charge of the meeting. For programs individual members gave demonstrations or talks on their projects. Often outside speakers were brought in to talk on subjects of interest to the members. There was always a beautifully planned Christmas party.

In the summer there were twilight meetings where the members toured the farms. Each child now had a chance to show off his project. The county agent or his assistant was always present to give pointers on grooming animals for the fair, and also pointers on showmanship, which were so very important. Just before the fair there was the big 4-H Club picnic when all the project reports had to be handed in.

Now came fair time when Herb Veness, with his big cattle truck, circled the prairie, picking up all the livestock. The boys and girls never forgot his patience and kindness. He was an honored guest at one of their banquets. As the cattle entered the fairgrounds the fun began. The first few hours were occupied with finding their places in the exhibit halls, cleaning up, arranging exhibits and making friends with boys and girls from other parts of the county.

The excitement mounted as the day of judging and showmanship arrived. The boys and girls from Eden Prairie always made a good showing with many going to the state fair. Some we remember who had state-fair trips were Ken and Tommy Anderson, Ward and Dean Holasek, Mary Ellen and Paul Anderson, Steve Roe and Dennis Nesbitt. We're sure we've missed the names of a few. Sorry.

Margaret Bren was the leader of the girls in dressmaking. Our girls took many prizes in the dress reviews at both the county and state level. Mildred Bren, with her musical leadership, organized a girls chorus which sang throughout the county. Elizabeth Marsh, with her artistc talent, helped with the fair booth and exhibits. She also helped with the scenery for the plays the group put on.

Some of our members won trips to the Junior Livestock Show in South St. Paul and the National Livestock Show in Chicago. Two won trips to Washington, D.C.: Ward Holasek and Donna Nesbitt.

We could go on and on about the merits of the 4-H Club and what it did for the boys and girls in Eden Prairie. We're just very grateful we had the opportunity to serve as local leaders.

Ralph and Marion Nesbitt

Everett McClay Post No. 409 Legion Hall on County Road 4.

American Legion, Everett McClay Post No. 409

Two returning World War I veterans can be credited with starting our local Legion post for they were already Legionnaires.

Arthur Miller was stationed in Washington, D.C. in the Quartermasters Corp. His brother, Harold, a Navy man, was also in Washington when the first Legion post in the United States was organized in 1918, the George Washington Post No. 1. Arthur and Harold joined this post and are charter members.

The local Legion post was organized in 1919 and received its charter on January 6, 1920. It was named after the first World War I casualty in the Eden Prairie-Bloomington area, Everett McClay.

The first meetings were held in the homes or in Miller's Hall above the Miller Brothers store. After the new consolidated school was opened the one-room schools were put up for sale. The Legion bought the Jarrett School for one hundred dollars. This was their headquarters for twenty-five years when it went up in smoke in 1940 from an overheated stove.

With the little insurance money, donated labor and many fund-raising projects, the Legion was able to build its present building near the railroad tracks on County Road 4.

As soon as the hall was built the Legion started holding the never-to-be-forgotten fish fries. Memories bring back the taste of the good potato salad, the coleslaw, the baked beans and all the fish one could eat for $1.25. Some of the faithful people in the kitchen were Fred and Ann Miller, Liz and Dewey Miller, Ella Moran, Dorothy and Lorman Jarrett, to name a few.

The Legion has done many things for the community of Eden Prairie. It is my desire to list a few: Boys and Girls State in cooperation with the school; scholarships and medals for outstanding seniors; sponsorship of a Boy Scout troop; aid with food and labor when tragedy has hit an Eden Prairie family; and foremost, the services provided each Memorial Day.

Harold Unze
Commander, 1956 and 1965

The Woman's Club

The club began as a class in child development and nutrition in 1930, using the University of Minnesota Extension courses as study material. The class numbered eight. Two of the original class are still club members: Mildred Tuckey and Marion Long.

In 1931 this group organized as the Mother's Club with Mrs. Roy Anderson serving as the first president. The purpose of the club is aptly stated in its creed:

We agree we ought to be better citizens and homemakers

and to this end we promise:
To do our best with any task assigned;
To be faithful in little things;
To be loyal to each other, avoiding petty jealousies, unfriendly criticism and gossip;
To pursue such studies as will help us keep pace with our home and community life;
As a member of the Woman's Club, I accept this as my creed.

The many projects and studies pursued by the club have furthered this purpose. The members have taken interesting field trips, have invited speakers to share ideas and expertise, have heard numerous book and play reviews, have explored one another's interests through their hobbies, have moved in local and national politics, and have explored history and geography as they have set up annual themes to follow in their more structured meetings.

In 1937 a Mothers Choral group was initiated under the direction of Mrs. Sherman Mitchell, wife of our school superintendent. This group sang at various places including the local churches, the PTA, the radio station WTCN, the Ladies Aid gatherings and the county and state PTA programs.

In 1938 the members changed the name to the Woman's Club, for they felt that some women who were not mothers might like to join. And many did.

This club will celebrate its fiftieth anniversary in 1981. The club creed still stands and has worn well through the years. Speaking for myself, it was the creed and the way I observed the members living that creed that kept me a loyal member. It's a group that has disciplined itself to think positively and lovingly of all members, that accepts variety in human nature, and benefits from that acceptance by appreciating each person's uniqueness and contribution as a whole. I am proud to be a member.

Elizabeth C. Bryan
Club Historian

Pretty Gals and Dashing Hats. Announcing the Eden Prairie Community Club Style Show at the Eden Prairie High School cafeteria, March 15, 1961. From left to right: Mrs. Howard Kaerwer, chairman; Mrs. George Adzick, president; Mrs. Leonard Holte, secretary. Hennepin County Review, March 16, 1961.

The Community Club

In 1948 a group of young women organized the Eden Prairie Junior Guild. Their programs emphasized homemaking and nutrition under the direction of the University of Minnesota Extension Division. A growing desire among the members to become a community service organization resulted in its becoming the Community Club in 1957. Membership was limited to forty so meetings could be held in the homes.

The club has sponsored, promoted and supported many worthwhile projects. They educated a little girl in India until she graduated from college as a public-health nurse. They provide tickets to the Minnesota Orchestra student concerts for students in the seventh and eighth grades. In the bicentennial year the club put on the Calico Ball at the new Eden Prairie Center.

Funds for their many activities have been raised by holding style shows and in more recent years by spring salad luncheons held in the fellowship hall of the Eden Prairie Presbyterian Church.

The club has taken a number of interesting tours. They have listened, learned and shared with many guest speakers. There is a common bond of friendship and service among its members.

Mildred Clark

Cub Scout Charles Schaitberger.

Girl Scouts. The leaders are Joy Brekke and Kay Roe.

Boy Scouts

In 1951 the first Cub pack and the first Scout troop were formed in Eden Prairie. They were first sponsored by the Eden Prairie School Parent Teacher Assocation and then by Everett McClay American Legion Post 409. Amos Gens was the first leader of Cub pack No. 242 and Gordon England was Eden Prairie's first Scoutmaster.

Scout Troop 242 has always been known as a "cooking troop." The boys made mud ovens and baked mouth-watering treats. They also demonstrated "tonka bakers" long before others knew of their existence. The troop excelled in pioneering and often put up towers and luxenbergers at district events. Funds for their activities were raised by putting on pancake breakfasts.

For a time there were Explorer posts in Eden Prairie. Kenneth Middleton advised a camping and ecology post while James Flavin and George Johnstone advised a scuba-diving post.

Allene Hookom

Girl Scouts

In approximately 1950 Mrs. Lorman (Dorothy) Jarrett asked Mrs. Sever (Martha) Peterson to go with her to a Girl Scout training session. Mrs. Jarrett had a troop at the Glen Lake Sanitarium at the time and Martha mentioned to Mrs. Harold (Betty) Schaitberger that it seemed unfair to have the Eden Prairie Scouts travel to Glen Lake to meet.

It was decided to have a wiener roast at the Hopperstadt home within walking distance of the Eden Prairie school. The roast was announced at school, and rather than a few girls attending, many boys and girls showed up for the free hot dogs. Although the food ran out, the women felt the kids were really expressing an interest in Scouting. The women fought for and received PTA sponsorship for Girl Scouting and Boy Scouting.

Betty and Martha assumed direction of the first troop, which was made up mostly of upper elementary girls. Three of the Scouts were Barbara Bren, Jackie Pavelka and

Maxine Boyd. Meanwhile, an organizational meeting was held at the Peterson home to find additional leaders, and soon after, a group of second graders was organized into Eden Prairie's first Brownie troop. While the Girl Scout troop lasted only a year, the first Brownie troop followed Scouting all the way through their senior year of high school. The troop was led by Mrs. Clyde (Kay) Roe and Mrs. Al (Joy) Brekke. Eight girls—Judy Moran, Susan Finholt, Zola Simons, Marlys Kaye, Joan Peterson, Barbara Roe, Sandy Wittenberg and Linda Brekke—remained in Scouting for the eleven-year program.

Round Lake became the site of the first Girl Scout day camp. Mrs. Jack (Mareth) Carter is credited with starting the camp around 1956. Field days were held on Purgatory Creek on the property of Mrs. George (Florence) Munier. The first Brownie box supper with fathers was held in conjunction with Hopkins at the Alice Smith School in Hopkins in 1952.

Linda Brekke Mona

PEOPLE AND
THINGS BEST REMEMBERED

This I Remember

My grandfather, James Anderson, lived in a big house where Sears south parking lot is today. I was only four year old when he died, but I can remember being in this house with many people walking around all dressed in black. From the front window I watched the long procession of black buggies slowly make its way to the Presbyterian Church and the Pleasant Hill Cemetery.

I was the same age when my father installed the electric lighting plant on our farm in 1912. My mother had lived in the city and this was what she missed most. The trade name was Globe Lighting Plant. This plant furnished our electricity until Northern States Power put in the highline in 1938. When I became old enough it was my job to operate the plant. It was a thirty-two volt direct current and consisted of sixteen batteries, each in separate glass cells. These batteries had to be replaced about every five years. It was run by a four-horsepower, one-cylinder Fuller and Johnson gas engine. This engine didn't have a muffler and made lots of noise. Every time it fired the lights would become brighter for an instant. These lights were a thrill for the whole neighborhood as we lived on a high hill and our three yard lights could be seen for a long distance. We even had a light in our little private outhouse.

I remember our trips to Shakopee with the horse and buggy or by sleigh in the winter. We'd stop at the spring (Miller's Spring) to water the horses. The water flowed through a culvert under the narrow road into a little stream on the other side. If there wasn't a can handy we'd scoop up the water in our hats or kneel down and drink direct. There was an Indian camp with several tepees and huts on the north side of the river. As the road ran along the river for a way, we had to pass this camp. It was a bit frightening as our adults used to tell us that if we didn't behave they would drop us off there. But the Indians were always friendly.

We crossed the river by the way of the old St. Louis Street bridge that was so constructed that it could open to let the riverboats through. The bridge was made of heavy planks that shrank in dry weather and rattled as the horses passed over them. My dad had spirited horses and they always sprang into action when we hit those planks. This really frightened me and was one of the reasons I never liked going to Shakopee.

We also made trips to Minneapolis with the horse and buggy as my grandmother, three uncles and an aunt lived there. In the winter we used the sleigh. The city kids liked to tie their sleds to the back of the sleigh or ride on the runners.

Josie, our hired girl, came directly from Bohemia. We contacted her through the Picha family. My parents sent money for her passage to America. Josie could not speak a word of English when she arrived but picked it up quickly as she was a very bright girl. Josie loved the cattle and horses and soon became a big help to my parents. She lived with us many years until she married and moved to Glencoe.

In 1916 we bought our first Model T Ford for four hundred dollars. My dad had a difficult time learning to drive. He smashed into a tree in our yard soon after he bought it. I can still hear him yelling, "Whoa," but it didn't stop.

Highway 5 was just a township road that was usually in poor condition. When a car passed that we could not recognize we'd call up all the neighbors to find out who it might be.

Our telephone service came from Shakopee and we paid the bill of twelve dollars once a year. There were seventeen on our party line. It was one of those wooden box phones that hung on the wall with a crank on the right side. I remember it was dangerous to use the phone during a storm as sparks would fly in all directions. Our call was two short, one long, and one short. News traveled fast as everyone on the line could hear our ring and listen in.

I remember the patriotic spirit of World War I with folks selling Liberty Bonds and Red Cross groups making bandages, knitting socks, mittens and sweaters. Many young men from Eden Prairie joined the 151st Division of the Rainbow. Many did not return and some suffered for years from the mustard gas used by the Germans. There was a false report on November 9, 1918 that the war was over. The school boards closed all the schools and we all celebrated until after November 11, when the Armistice was signed. When the 151st Division returned, we all went to Minneapolis to watch the big parade down Nicollet Avenue. Bands played and the church bells rang.

When the Barnum and Bailey or Ringling Brothers Circus came to Minneapolis most of the people in Eden Prairie went to see it. There was the big parade up Nicollet Ave-nue in the morning and then the big performance in the afternoon. Admission was fifty cents for adults and ten cents for children. As kids in the country had to create their own fun, we'd come home and put on our own circus.

One time we gathered up the neighborhood kids and put together a circus that became a big attraction. It was held at our house. There were the Watkins and Perkl kids and Doug Benson. Our cousin, Dave Johnson of Minneapolis, was the ringmaster. The parents had as much fun as the kids. The Watkins pony led the parade. Her head and ears were decorated with colored paper. A small dog that also was dressed up rode on her back. There was the big dog that pulled the wagon with the dressed-up pig on it. We had several clowns. The admission was two cents. Our parents put in enough extra money to make ten dollars, which we gave to the Red Cross. The Minneapolis Journal got word of this event and our giving ten dollars to help win the war. They published a short article about our circus in their paper. So we had to give a repeat performance two weeks later. This time things didn't go so well. More kids wanted to get in on it. The pony bucked and reared. The dog fell off, frightening the other animals. Although things got off to a bad start, it still was a success and this time we had twenty-five dollars for the Red Cross.

Eden Prairie had its dark days. In 1919, during the flu epidemic, the sting of death swept the town. Many homes were left motherless. Then on June 3, 1925, a tornado hit, blowing down nineteen barns and destroying many smaller farm buildings in its path of destruction. In the mid-1930s came the terrible heat wave and drought. The hottest day was 108 degrees. The heat was so intense that farmers could not work their horses during the day and many got up at two o'clock and worked until mid-morning.

I remember how we rebelled against the first game warden who patrolled Eden Prairie. It really got us when we couldn't shoot pheasants on our own farms when we wanted to or spear a few northerns in Purgatory Creek in the spring. Sometimes Art Watkins, my neighbor pal, and a few other young fellows would play tricks on the game warden. We'd call and say we heard shooting at the other end of the town. Then we'd have an hour or more of good shooting. There were thousands of pheasants in Eden Prairie in the 1930s and '40s.

The years have brought many changes to Eden Prairie, some for the best. I do miss the beautiful dairy herds grazing in the pastures and on the hillsides. It has bothered me to see the fields grow up in weeds. These weeds used to be destroyed before they went to seed. I miss the friendship and loyalty to each other that existed among the farmers and how they all pitched in to help each other in times of trouble. Those working bees I'll never forget. One time Loring Tuckey was too ill to work his fields. About a dozen tractors showed up. The Gordon Smith Oil Company came and filled them all with gas. All of Loring's fields were plowed in half a day. That's the spirit of Eden Prairie that I want to remember.

Calvin Anderson

Hobos

There were hoboes, or tramps as some called them, riding the empty railroad cars. Many lived in the empty boxcars on the side tracks at the Eden Prairie station. Some didn't have any place in particular to go while others were getting free transportation between jobs.

They'd often start a little fire and heat coffee in an old coffee can. We'd have to watch carefully to see they didn't start a nearby field on fire.

When they came to the store for a handout my dad would always send them out to the woodpile to split wood for while before my mother gave them a good meal.

One day my dad told me to go up in the haymow and pitch down some hay for the horses. I stuck the fork into the hay and a man yelled out. It didn't take me long to scram out of there. My dad then went up there and got the same response. A man then came out from under the hay and said, "Please let me sleep here for the night. I'm awfully sick." My dad said, "If you're a sick man come over to the store."

They found the man really was sick. They set up a cot for him by the stove in the hall above the store. Mother called Dr. Smith from Shakopee, who found the man had pneumonia. Mother cared for him for more than two weeks. One day he came down the stairs, thanked Mother, and was on his way again.

Arthur Miller

The Gypsies

The nomadic Gypsies also wandered through Eden Prairie. The people feared them, yet were fascinated by them.

It was exciting to see the Gypsies every summer as they camped along Purgatory Creek below our farm where the Mr. Steak restaurant is today. They usually had three or four wagons and stayed four or five days. Sometimes in dry weather they'd soak their wagon wheels in the creek so the wood would expand and tighten the iron rims of the wheels.

They'd come up the hill to the house and ask to buy eggs but seldom paid for them. We'd have to watch the chicken coop for they'd swipe eggs, chickens, and feed for their horses. We'd see them cutting hay with a scythe at the edge of our hay field.

I thought the men, with their black hair and dark brown eyes, were very handsome. They wore red bandanas around their necks. The women were gaily dressed and wore big aprons.

Usually the town constable would have to come and see them on their way.

Calvin Anderson

The Gypsies often camped by our Miller's Spring on Spring Road. First they came in wagons and then later in old cars. They were dark-skinned and wore colorful clothes. The women wore big aprons and many skirts.

The cry from all the neighbors was, "The Gypsies are coming!" They'd all run to protect their belongings. They would come into our store. We'd have to watch carefully or they'd sweep everything off the shelves.

One time my mother had all the food on the table for dinner. She left the room for a few minutes. A group of Gypsy women came in and took everything on the table, putting it in their big aprons.

The women were always telling fortunes. One time Jim Stewart was taken in by one of these women. A short time later, when he put his hand in his pocket he found his money was gone.

Arthur Miller

Salesmen and Peddlers

Salesmen were always driving up to the kitchen door and trying to sell something. I remember an insurance man who came once a year. He'd feed his horse, eat a meal with us and stay overnight. He wrote up our insurance but I don't remember if we got a discount for his night accommodation.

Abbie Tuckey Picha

A clothing salesman used to come to our house. His buggy was piled with suitcases. He always stayed overnight. Before he left in the morning, he'd give my Dad a new shirt.

It was an old saying that some salesmen arranged to arrive near dinnertime at the homes where they could be assured a good meal.

Calvin Anderson

Some peddlers would drive in the yard in old wagons drawn by skinny horses. Some of those horses were so skinny one could see every rib in their body. They'd ask to buy old rags and all the old junk they might see around the place.

I remember one man who came around selling meats. He always had a frail little girl beside him in the buggy.

Beatrice Glenn Veness

There were men going around selling nursery stock and seeds. One seed salesman introduced that obnoxious weed, leafy spurge, to Eden Prairie. The leafy spurge seeds were mixed with some of the seed he sold. The farmers battled that weed in their fields for years. There are still plenty of those yellow flowering plants around today but nobody cares, for they aren't farming.

We had salesmen from the Grand Union Tea and Coffee Company and the Jewel Tea Company stop at our house. There was a blind man and his companion from Cologne who came around once a year selling brooms and brushes.

Priscilla Blakeborough Good

I think we all used the products sold by the Watkins and Raleigh salesmen. There was one salesman from Excelsior by the name of Windsor. He was such a nice man. Then Charlie Phillips was our Raleigh man for many years. These men sold all the farm and home remedies one could think of. They had horse liniments, ointments for wounds and sores, lice powder for the chickens, cough syrups, salves, pills, spices, vanilla, nectar and all kinds of beauty aids. It was exciting to see them open up their big suitcases and show off their products.

Eva Klima Hirt

Monroe Barker

Monroe was a Negro boy who was born and lived in the South. After the Civil War, with a large number of other slaves, he was boarded into a boxcar and shipped north into Missouri. He didn't know what his name was, who or where his parents were, and he couldn't read or write.

In Missouri he wandered from place to place until he met Jonas Staring from Eden Prairie. Staring had bought a horse and was having it shipped to Eden Prairie. He asked Monroe to ride in the car with the horse to take care of it.

was a member of the family. If he so wished he could wait and be served later with what was left. The salesman quickly found his place at the table.

The four Miller brothers grew to manhood and started farming. Their father told them that surely they could find work for Mun. He had a wonderful way with horses and soon took on the job of tending to the teams. Some of the horses were hard to handle but Mun could walk into a stall with any of the horses and they never threatened him while one of the boys would have been kicked through the door.

Monroe Barker's tombstone in the Eden Prairie Cemetery on County Road 4.

Mun—the name he soon was to be known by—made his home with the Starings for a time and then moved on to another family, the Rankins. Soon he was adrift again and Fred Miller, father of the four Miller boys, welcomed him into his home. Fred Miller saw to it that Monroe always had work with the nearby farmers who probably paid him a dollar a day, the going rate.

Since the Millers owned a store, there were many salesmen stopping from time to time. Fred's wife, Kate, would always ask them to eat with them. One day one of the salesmen remarked, as he saw Mun take his place at the table, that he didn't dine with Negroes, whereupon Kate Miller told him that Mun

As Mun didn't know his age or birthday, Mrs. Miller said that February 12 would be as good a date as any. How he got his name was not known. He was liked by everyone. He knew his place and was always very much a gentleman. When he came to Eden Prairie he was a big, six-foot man, but in later years, due to illness, he became short and stooped.

One day Mun became very ill. Mrs. Miller took care of him as though he was one of the family. He didn't last long. His death came in March, 1942. He was thought to be more that one hundred years old. The funeral was at the Miller home. There was a big crowd, for he had many friends.

Before he died, Mun bought a cemetery lot and had a granite monument with his name erected there. There are no dates, for he didn't know his birth date nor, of course, the day he was to die.

Near his grave rest many Millers because, you see, Mun left all his possessions, including the lot and a few hundred dollars, to Kate Miller, the lovely lady who had been his friend.

Dotty D. Nye

(Miss Nye taught in the Eden Prairie Schools for twenty-five years and boarded with the Miller family until Kate Miller's death in 1950.)

Old Joe

Old Joe, as he affectionately was called, had been a slave boy in the South. No one seems to know how he came to Eden Prairie. He first lived with the Frank Rivers family and then moved on to my grandfather's house, the Horace Goodrich home. For a time he drove horses for Dr. Fisher in Shakopee as the doctor made his house calls.

When my uncle, John Goodrich, built his big house that soon opened as a summer hotel on Staring Lake, Joe went to live with him. He helped around the hotel, cared for the lawn and boats, worked around the kitchen and helped the guests with their luggage. He drove the surrey with the fringe on top that picked up guests at the Eden Prairie station.

Old Joe lived with our families until the infirmities of old age took his life. He was buried in the Eden Prairie Cemetery. A little wooden cross marked the grave. My Father made a fine marker for the grave but for some unknown reason it was never erected in the cemetery.

As time passed, the grass grew up and there was no sign of Old Joe's grave, but the sextons of the cemetery to this day know the approximate location and keep the area well mowed. There is an understanding that Old Joe's resting place will never be disturbed.

Helen Goodrich Mastin

Rodeo Riders.

Horses, Horses, Horses

For the kids in Eden Prairie who liked horses, George and Ruby Boyd were very special people. They had a farm on Duck Lake Trail. George bought and sold horses, boarded horses and gave riding lessons. They had four daughters—Patsy, Maxine, Winifred and Terry. All the girls were top riders.

Each summer a group of kids who had riding horses would meet at the Boyd place and practice for a rodeo which was put on in the early part of September. This went on for years. I was about eight years old when I started going up there and it kept on until I graduated from high school.

The Roderick twins, Bryan and Brent, and their little sister, Marcia, lived at the junction of Highways 169 and 5. They used to ride up Highway 5 on their horses. Mary Ellen Anderson joined them at the bottom of her hill. My sister, Carol, and I would be waiting at the School Road. We'd all go clip clop over the railroad bridge to County Road 4, then north to the little road that goes past Prairie View School to Duck Lake Trail. Here, Gordy Stodola and Johnny Hughes would join us. By the time we got to Boyd's there were twenty or more horses and kids.

Patsy Boyd, being the oldest, was the coordinator and trainer. She kept us all in line. Her dad was so good to us. He tightened all our girths to make sure our saddles were securely in place. We all brought bag lunches but Ruby always brought out cold drinks and cookies or cake. We practiced all day from about ten o'clock in the morning until four o'clock in the afternoon. We never seemed concerned about riding home along Highway 5 around five o'clock in the afternoon.

Before the day of the rodeo the parents pitched in to help put up the viewing stand and benches around the corral. My dad always got a popcorn machine. We sold popcorn, cotton candy and pop. Admission was ten cents or any amount one wished to give. The money went to a charity like the Home for Retarded Children or the Cancer Fund.

Some of the events in the rodeo were square dancing, trick riding, pick-up races, barrel races and calf riding. Patsy Boyd often played her guitar and sang western songs. We had a number of clowns. Friends from Minneapolis and the surrounding communities came to watch us.

Another big event was to take our horses to Hopkins and ride in the Raspberry Parade. Some kids rode in the horse shows at the county fair.

We had so much fun riding the back trails around Mitchell Lake. After one of these rides a real tragedy occurred. Mary Ellen Anderson's dad had told her to never leave her horse untied in a pasture with other horses for they sometimes get jealous and would start fighting. One time we thoughtlessly left the horses untied in our pasture when we went to the house for a little lunch. Soon we could hear a great commotion in the pasture. My horse and Carol's horse had chased Mary Ellen's palomino, Pixie, into the barbed-wire fence. There she stood in a pool of blood. We ran to the house to get rags for a tourniquet and got Balfanz's horse trailer to take her home. The people who gathered around the horse said there was only one thing to do and that was to shoot the horse for she'd never walk again. Mary Elllen would not hear of that and Dr. Wright was called, Mary Ellen nursed Pixie during the day and got up twice during the night. With care and many prayers, Pixie's leg did heal. She wasn't as frisky as before but was still a good rider. Dr. John Wright was a special friend to all the little girls in Eden Prairie who loved horses.

Diane Dredge Simons

Thanksgiving Days Spent in Church

Thanksgiving and a day in church used to be synonymous in the minds of members of the Eden Prairie Presbyterian Church.

On Thanksgiving morning the whole family —including city cousins, other relatives and friends—piled into the buggy or the car in later years and headed for the church and a day of togetherness.

The day began with a worship service, which was followed by the Thanksgiving dinner and an afternoon of visiting for the elders and fun and games for the youngsters.

The women of the church began preparing for Thanksgiving Day many weeks in advance. One of their favorite projects was a "friendship quilt." Each member of the Ladies Aid took a square to quilt and embroider with names.

It cost ten cents to have your name put on the quilt. After each completed her square, the quilt was assembled. It was auctioned off Thanksgiving Day, with the proceeds going to the church. Mildred Tuckey has one of these quilts that belonged to her mother.

The women also prepared baked and canned goods and turned out a variety of handmade items for the bazaar in the church parlor.

The main feature of the day, however, was the dinner. The long tables virtually sagged under all the food. The turkeys were fresh out of the farm yard, plucked and cleaned by the women at the church and then taken back home to be baked to a taste-tempting golden brown.

Stuffing was whipped up by the washtub full. Baked squash, cranberries and coleslaw were plentiful. Homemade apple or pumpkin pie was offered to those who had room for dessert.

Today (the old church building on Pioneer Trail is gone) no longer do the families spend the day in church.

But the memories of those days linger on to warm the hearts of those of us who remember this Thanksgiving Day.

Abbie Tuckey Picha

Celebrating Christmas

Christmas meant bundling up on a silent night for an hour's ride to Shakopee for a church service. We rode in sleds with big boxes that had straw on the bottom. The snow used to twinkle and it was just beautiful.

There were no sounds but the bells on the horses. The ride was smooth—no bumps—because there was so much snow back then. The air was so fresh, but once in a while we'd smell the horses.

Our little church—we thought it was big then—had a huge Christmas tree that touched the ceiling. There were real candles on the tree. Pails of water were set around the tree in case it caught on fire.

The tree at home also had candles on it. We children were not allowed to light them unless Father or Mother were around. One time I lit the candles when Mother was gone, but she returned and put the fire out before there was any damage. I hid in the closet and never did that again.

On Christmas Eve we'd hurry to finish our chores. The church service started at 6 p.m. and lasted until 7:30. It was about 8:30 by the time we got home and found Santa Claus had been there, bringing the tree and gifts.

We never saw any decorations before Christmas Eve and often wondered how the tree and presents got there while we were in church. We got few toys and more practical gifts such as hand-knitted scarves, mittens and stockings. One Christmas I got a doll. It had a china head and hands with eyes that opened and closed with real eyelashes. I had this doll a long time but one day a friend came over and dropped it. The head broke.

We always had oyster stew made with the quart of oysters that Millers store gave its customers for Christmas. Rice pudding, oranges, apples and hard candy were also among the holiday treats.

The week between Christmas and New Year's Day was a time for socializing. We'd bundle up again and hop in the sleigh for a ride to relatives and friends. There were no carolers who went from house to house in those days for the houses were too far apart. But whenever a group got together we'd sing carols.

I think my mother worked as hard as any mother today does in preparing for Christmas, but I think she enjoyed it more. It was more of a fun time. Now people are so busy and full of tension they can't enjoy it.

Louise Tessmer Mitchell

My Elephant From India

We lived on the old Indian trail that ran along the Minnesota River. On the north side of our house were high bluffs that followed the river in Eden Prairie.

For a number of years a tall, thin man came walking over these bluffs. He seemed to be well educated. Often he would stop in and visit with my grandfather, Harry Raquet.

On his last visit with us he turned to me and said, "I am going to India. What would you like me to send you?" I was only eight years old and all I knew about India was that elephants lived there. So I answered, "Send me an elephant."

The following Christmas, a brown paper package arrived in the mail. In the package was a little elephant and a note which just said, "From John in India."

I've treasured this little elephant. It has a special place on my fireplace mantel. But I've never stopped wondering who John was, what he did, why he loved the river bluffs in Eden Prairie and why he went to India.

Dorothy Raguet Doughty

Two Eminent Native Sons

From every community, men go forth into the wideness of the world, and their footprints carry the clay of their native soil. Eden Prairie, also, has many favorite sons and daughters. People who have made strong, singular contributions in government, science, and the arts. People who have shaped and are continuing to shape history.

Two Eden Prairie men who exemplify this process are Dr. Robert Page, and Duane Hulbert.

Dr. Robert Morris Page

Robert Morris Page was one of eleven children born into the family of Lily and Clarence Q. Page, who settled in Eden Prairie in 1909. C. Q. Page was active in civic affairs, and as president of the School Board was credited with effecting the school consolidation which closed the one-room schools and built the first central Eden Prairie School.

Dr. Robert Morris Page.

Robert Page entered Hamline University intending to study for the ministry, as had his father before him. A perceptive physics professor, however, recognized his scientific ability, and influenced him toward a career in physics. Hamline University later awarded him a Doctor of Science degree, and established an electronics laboratory in his name; a name that became known throughout the scientific world. For Robert Morris Page went on to complete graduate work at George Washington University in Washington, D.C., to perform research at the Naval Research Laboratory there, and to build the country's first pulse radar system. He invented the basic circuits of pulse radar, the radar duplexer, radar guidance of missiles, monopause precision tracking radar, very long range over-the-horizon radar, and the magnetic drum receiving equipment data processing system.

Dr. Page holds more than 60 patents in the field of radar, including substantially all basic radar patents.

At the time of his retirement (1966), he was Director of the Naval Research Laboratory, heading a staff of 1500 scientists, engineers, and technicians. He was honored by three presidents, including the President's Award for Distinguished Federal Civilian Service—the highest honor bestowed on career civil service employees—by President Dwight D. Eisenhower, in 1960.

In a letter, President Lyndon Johnson told Dr. Page, "Your distinguished career as a scientist and an administrator is an example for many dedicated young people who have chosen the public service as a career."

Duane Hulbert

Duane Hulbert, the great grandson of two early Eden Prairie residents, Charles and Losetta Goodrich Hulbert, is carrying the names of his family and community into the world of music, a different discipline than those chosen by his forebearers. For Charles Hulbert was a state senator, Duane Hulbert's grandfather, Howard Hulbert, was in agriculture, and his father, Lloyd Hulbert, an aeronautical instruments technician.

Musical gifts were prominent in both the Goodrich and Hulbert families, however, and so heritage had a part when Duane Hulbert played a piano concerto with the

Duane Hulbert.

University of Minnesota Orchestra at age 12, and won a Young Artists Competition sponsored by the Minnesota Orchestra at age 15. These were the beginning of many awards and scholarships, including the Schubert Club and Thursday Musical competitions, the Cleveland Institute of Music, Cleveland, Ohio, the Aspen Music Festival in Colorado, and the Julliard School of Music in New York. Having completed both Bachelors and Masters degrees at Julliard, he has been a student of the great Sascha Gorodnitzki, and is presently working on a doctorate. Mr. Hulbert has been guest artist with the Minnesota, North Carolina, and Portland Maine Symphony Orchestras, and winner of the Julliard Concerto Competition in 1978. Of that occasion, the New York Daily News reviewer wrote, ". . . the best performance of this concerto I have ever heard. I wish that the composer had been there to hear it."

Carol Quam Hone

The Rowland Ridge Farm that was at 13500 West 78th Street.

The Best of Two Worlds

They put down roots—their own and those of crops. They called the farms places with perhaps more meaning than they knew. There was Uncle David's place and Uncle Robert's place. High on a hill overlooking the big valley south of Highway 5 was John W.'s place. This was our home. We called it Rowland Ridge, meaning high and low in Scotland. When I came there people were enjoying country living with all the advantages of urban living within their reach. It was the best of two worlds.

The 1940s was a period of extensive remodeling of farmhouses. The challenge was to try to retain the charm of the past with modernization. Walls were removed to create an openness. Picture windows were added to let the beauty of the outdoors in. Now one could watch the sunrise from the kitchen table and the sunset from a living-room chair. Fireplaces, the pioneer's only means of heat, were brought back just to create a more cozy atmosphere. Paneled walls and wall-to-wall carpeting were new. Places were found for all types of time-saving appliances from fryers to dryers.

Life was rich and full if one chose to make it so. One could call the county library and find his favorite books at the local library within a few days. Entertainment of one's choice was just twenty minutes away in the Twin Cities. A longing for the academic life could be fulfilled for the University of Minnesota was just a half hour away. With the church, the school and an active woman's club, what more could one ask for?

The country provided room for privacy. The need to be alone and think one's own thoughts could be found in a walk through the big woods with all its soft, natural noises: branches of the trees brushing each other gently, birds singing in the treetops and all the little earth animals with their squeaks and chirps. We lived on a high hill but to the back of our place was a hill twice as high. Often I'd climb to the very top of this hill and quietly sit in the twilight as the lights of Edina, Shakopee and Chanhassen came on. I enjoyed the emotions of the outdoors, like finding the first wild flowers in spring or showing the children a nest of robin's eggs in the old crabapple tree.

Living in the country and on a farm was unique in that it was a family enterprise where even the children played an essential roll. It was a life when not completely embraced could cause great unhappiness. It didn't take long to find out you were your husband's business partner and shared the day-to-day problems and successes. There was little chance for alienation, for the whole family worked together to make the farm operation complete.

We were one with the farm and a part of the cycle of seasons. Spring brought tilling and seeding, summer hay-making and threshing, while the fall was spent stuffing barns and silos with the same vigor as the little squirrel filling his hole. Soon winter was upon us and the soil again rested beneath the snow.

Nature tempers a farmer with favors and failures. She could be absolutely indiscriminate in her actions at times. She could send a hailstorm that would just dampen one field while completely destroy another. There was always too much or not enough rain, a late spring or an early frost. But there always seemed to run a stream of optimism through it all and each new spring brought hope that this year would be a good one.

A farm was the ideal place to raise a family. Because there were no close next-door neighbors, a special closeness existed between sister and brother. Then the children could be with their father a lot and that was important. They learned to feel valuable as they shared the work of the farm. It was easy to talk about God, for creation was all around them. One did not have to invent situations to teach thrift, industry and perseverance. A 4-H heifer could take care of that.

The children lived a nearly ideal life of joy and freedom. In spring there were the trips

up Purgatory Creek to the beaver dam in the old duck boat. On the way they could quietly observe the many woodland creatures and birds in the thick underbrush on the banks of the stream. There were the big northerns that came upstream in the spring to spawn. How they did enjoy catching little turtles and crayfish.

There was Mama Cat with her litter after litter of kittens and Smoky, the Labrador, who always hid her pups in the hay. Oh, the joy in the faces of the children when they found them, waited for their eyes to open, and then taught them how to drink out of a dish. Yes, and there was great sorrow in giving them up for others wanted puppies from a dog with Smoky's hunting record. Then there is the memory of Father awakening the little sleepyheads early in the morning and then following him through the morning dew to the pasture where one of the riding horses stood with a new colt with wobbling legs by her side. The little one had already found its source of nourishment. Then there was riding through the woods and over the hills. The two hundred acres were their kingdom and the big farmhouse was the "castle on the hill."

The children learned about the seasons and all living things' relationship to them. They grew up with a special attitude toward animals, cared about them and learned their ways. It was this close relationship with a father who took the time to walk the fields and woods with his little girl, Mary Ellen, that ultimately led her into the study of biology and a Ph.D. in the field of ecology and animal behavior.

Occasionally, new tractors appeared on the hill. Each one was bigger than the one before. The last one was a huge, powerful, green-and-yellow John Deere. The children christened it the "Green Giant."

I can still see our young son going over its mechanism carefully with thoughts of some day getting behind that big wheel. The day came. I protested but his father said he was ready. I remember going day after day to a little knoll by the field where I could watch but not be seen. From this secret vantage point I watched my son go up and down the hills on the big monster. I was called foolish but I couldn't help it.

Time passed. The children went off to college. The state highway department wanted the front part of our place for the new, proposed Highway 169 to Shakopee that has never been built. The Rowland Ridge sign with the picture of Mary Ellen's palomino came down. For my husband it was just like uprooting a sturdy oak—roots that went back to the time his grandfather purchased the land after the treaty with the Indians.

How could the memory of the place be preserved? I had an artist acquaintance paint a large picture that encompassed the creek, the winding road up the hill, the two houses, the barn, the silo, and the windmill. It was a gift for our first Christmas in our new home on Topview Road. Naturally, my husband was touched, but the children exclaimed in one voice, "Who gets that picture when you two are gone?" My frugal ways weighed the situation and then putting true value in perspective, I ordered another painting.

When our son, Paul, set up his law practice he came to me and asked, "Mom, may I hang one of those paintings of the farm in my office?" I knew then how much his childhood home meant to him. It hangs in front of his desk where he can occasionally look and relax in past memories.

One can never fully come away from the land and the physical and spiritual experiences of childhood. Neither can one go back in time or space, but if we are lucky and wise we can use the things we've learned to help understand what we've become and why.

Eden Prairie is well into its second one hundred years. The rural farming era has closed and with it has gone much of its natural simplicity. It is now a city and one of the fastest-growing communities in the metropolitan area. City officials have stressed developments that blend with its natural beauty among the woods, lakes and streams, and have worked hard to protect these natural amenities so that the people who make Eden Prairie their home can also feel that they, too, are living in the best of two worlds.

Helen Holden Anderson

REFERENCES

The Aborigines of Minnesota. By N. H. Winchell, Minnesota Historical Society, St. Paul, 1967.

Agriculture. Roots, Volume 2, Number 2. Winter 1974, Minnesota Historical Society, St. Paul.

Alexander Wilkins - Secretary of the Minnesota Territory, Alexander Wilkins papers, Minnesota State Archives, Minnesota Historical Society, St. Paul.

Anderson Family Descent from 1575 to 1900. By Josiah M. Anderson, University Press, Minneapolis, 1900.

Anderson Geneology. Researched by Truman J. Beggs, Dallas, Texas. 1967.

Autobiography of Mary Jane Hill Anderson (1827-1924) - Written in her ninety-fifth year. Agnes Anderson Twitchell, 65 Bedford Street, Minneapolis, 1934.

Bloomington Historic Sites. By George E. Hopkins, Copyrighted 1968.

"Bohemian Immigration". By Ester Jerobek, a clipping from the Hennepin County Review, April 26, 1934, Hopkins Historical Society, Hopkins, Minnesota.

Burial Mounds of Central Minnesota. By Floyd A. Wilford. Eldon Johnson, and Joan Vicinus, Minnesota Historical Society, St. Paul, 1969.

Carrying the Mails of the United States in the State of Minnesota from July 1, 1895 to June 30, 1899. By W. S. Bissell, Postmaster General, Washington Printing Office, 1894.

"Citizens League Meeting", a clipping from the Hennepin County Review, March 2, 1961, Eden Prairie Historical Society.

Dahcotah - Life and Legend of the Sioux Around Fort Snelling. By Mrs. Mary Henderson Eastman (1818-1890). Ross and Haines, Inc. Minneapolis, 1962.

Eden Prairie Cemetery Association Report, Compiled by Homer Raguet, February 10, 1974.

Eden Prairie - Land Owners of Eden Prairie Township. Book of Abstracts, Hennepin County Courthouse, Minneapolis, 1879.

Eden Prairie Presbyterian Church Centennial Booklet, 1956.

Eden Prairie Presbyterian Church Dedication Service, June 26, 1960.

Eden Prairie Schools - From the Little Log Schools to Consolidated School District 141. By Helen H. Anderson, Eden Prairie Historical Society.

"Eden Prairie Town Meeting" a clipping from the Hennepin County Review, March 16, 1961, Eden Prairie Historical Society.

Eden Prairie Twsp 116, Range 22 - First Purchasers and Settlers, First Book of Abstracts, Hennepin County Courthouse, Minneapolis, 1855.

Eden Prairie United Methodist Church - 115 Anniversary Booklet, With an Introduction by Rev. Aldon W. Keiski, 1970.

Eden Prairie United Methodist Church - 125 Anniversary, May 21, 1978.

Education in Minnesota. Roots, Volume 2, Number 2. Fall 1973, Minnesota Historical Society, St. Paul.

Emigration. Roots, Volume 1, Number 3. Spring 1973, Minnesota Historical Society, St. Paul.

Farm Journal - 100 Years of Farm Journal. Countryside Press, Philadelphia, Pennsylvania, 1976.

Gopher Historian (selections). Poatgieter and Dunn, ed. Minnesota Historical Society, St. Paul.

Hennepin County History Magazine, 1958-1964. Hennepin County Historical Society, Minneapolis.

History of the Diocese of Minnesota - Fifty Years of Church Work in Minnesota, 1857-1909, Dedicated to Rt. Rev. H. B. Whipple, First Bishop of the State of Minnesota. By Rev. George C. Tanner, D. D., 1907.

History of Hennepin County and the City of Minneapolis. By the Reverend Edward D. Neill, North Star Publishing Co., Minneapolis, 1881.

History of the Minnesota Valley. By the Reverend Edward D. Neill, North Star Publishing Co. Minneapolis, 1882.

History of Steamboating on the Minnesota River. By Thomas Hughes, Minnesota Historical Society Collections, Volume 10, Part 1. Minnesota Historical Society, St. Paul. 1905.

Hulbert Diary of Yearly Events from 1900-1936. Eden Prairie Historical Society.

Indians of Minnesota, Compiled by the Minnesota Historical Society, St. Paul.

Isaac Crowe - Letters and Records, Minnesota State Archives, Minnesota Historical Society, St. Paul.

The Land Lies Open. By Theodore C. Blegen, University of Minnesota Press, Minneapolis, 1949.

Manufacture of Pottery in Minnesota. By C. Hubert Smith, Minnesota Archaeologist, Volume 36, Number 4. December 1977, Minnesota Historical Society, St. Paul.

Old Rail Fence Corners. By Lucy Leavenworth Wilder Morris, ed. 1914.

Personal Recollections of Minnesota and Its People and Early History of Minneapolis, By John H. Stevens, Tribune Job Printing Co. Minneapolis, 1890

"Pioneer of Prairie Recalls Log Cabin and Ox Cart Days - Edward Gamble", a clipping from the Hennepin County Review, December 5, 1929, Eden Prairie Historical Society.

Pleasant Hill Cemetery Association Report, Compiled by Beatrice Veness, February 10, 1974, Eden Prairie Historical Society.

"Prairie Fights to Hold Post Office", a clipping from the Hennepin County Review, September 6, 1934, Eden Prairie Historical Society.

Railroads in the Days of Steam. Published by American Heritage, Harper, 1960.

Railroads in the Story of Minnesota. Gopher Historian, Volume 25, Number 3. Minnesota Historical Society, St. Paul.

Rocking in the Cradle of Minnesota Agriculture. Written by the Agricultural Classes of the Hopkins High School under the direction of Dr. V. E. Nylon, 1933-34, Hopkins Historical Society, Hopkins, Minnesota.

"Saw Battle Near City". By Myron S. Staring, a clipping from the Minneapolis Journal, June 12, 1915, Tuttle Collections, Hennepin County Historical Society, Minneapolis.

The Shakopee Story. By Julius A. Coller, II, North Star Pictures, Inc. Shakopee, 1960.

The Sioux Uprising of 1862. By Kenneth Carley, Minnesota Historical Society, St. Paul.

"The Stewart Family", a clipping from the Hennepin County Review, December 5, 1929, Hopkins Historical Society, Hopkins, Minnesota.

Summer Rambles in the West. By Elizabeth Fry Ellet, J. C. Fiker, New York, 1853.

"Town Meeting For Eden Prairie Might Be Last One As Township", a clipping from the Hennepin County Review, March 9, 1961, Eden Prairie Historical Society.

Walk Beside the River of Tomorrow - A Prophecy. By Mrs. Robert Lucas, Written for the Thirty-Seventh Anniversary and Jubilee Service of the Macomber Memorial Methodist Episcopal Church, Eden Prairie, June 6, 1909.

"Veteran Eden Prairie Carrier Quits October 1 - Harry S. Neill, a clipping from the Hennepin County Review, October 4, 1934, Eden Prairie Historical Society.

The information contained in this book is as accurate as possible with existing available research material.